Table

Foreword

Sooner or later, everything comes back into fashion.
Casting about for a definition of magic, you could do worse than: "Magic is the act of locating and then claiming your place in the universe." Any further elaboration beyond such a statement is, more often than not, merely a personal commentary.

It is that *claiming* of your place that concerns us here. Practical enchantment. Where the rubber meets the road. Where the pump meets the runway.

Enter glamour.

Glamour involves augmenting the aspect of yourself that needs to be top of its game for you to achieve your desired end. Glamour does not live in the first class lounge. It does not look like the Koh-i-noor diamond. It does not smell like the 1%. Rather, it hangs in the air when most of the guests have left the party. It's just you, your friends, and some expiring candles. It summons your attention to the restaurant door as a girl who just has *something* enters. It talks the traffic cop out of giving you that fine. Glamour is ephemeral and situational. It is not prosaic like mere wealth or beauty.

Near the root of Italy's current troubles as well as its possible salvation is the notion -beloved in the south, particularly- of *la bella figura*, or 'beautiful figure'. This is the idea of putting your best foot forward regardless of your circumstances. It means making the best aesthetic impression you possibly can. It includes a mandatory pantomime of style, civility and confidence.

Whilst the outward manifestation of glamour displays some casual similarities, glamour runs deeper than surface appearances... much deeper. It is *la bella figura degli Dei*. It is more than merely changing out of your sweat suit before going to the market. It is a set of multidimensional brand guidelines.

Getting closer to the subject than 'guidelines' presents some challenges. If it didn't, you would be holding in your hand an index card rather than an entire book. My favourite bar in the Bastille area of Paris, La Rotonde, is, in many ways, unremarkable. However, it stays open late. You can sit out the front, drinking your way down the cocktail list and watching the French have minor road accidents at the very small roundabout just in front of you that gives the place its name. One rainy evening, spying that the place was unusually quiet, we stopped off for a few drinks on the walk home from supper. Several hours later, after politely enduring my terrible French, the waiters started bringing out round after round of complementary, experimental cocktails in little test tubes. What followed was an entirely unanticipated and *glamorous* late evening watching the beautiful denizens of the Parisian night leap into their second life. There is no precise formula for the evocation of glamour. The best you can do is invite it and cross your fingers.

This is as it should be, for *caprice* lives close to the heart of practical enchantment. Glamour's potency lies in the inconstancy of its application. How could it be otherwise? Even your heirloom diadem will lose its lustre if you wear it while cleaning the bathroom.

Sitting alongside capriciousness is another similarly dangerous and intoxicating aspect of glamour: *deception*. While it is true that glamour is deployed to augment existing characteristics, glamour is also used in the deliberate creation of wholesale illusion. These are the arts of the marginalised, the hidden. Cinderella was politically isolated not only because she was a woman, but also because she was a woman of very little means. A monarch has the option of lopping off displeasing heads. A serving girl must achieve her ends in subtler ways.

So from this perspective, glamour is not exclusively feminine. However, it is entirely *fae*. Glamour is the principal modus operandi of the Secret Commonwealth. Perhaps a good example of this not-always-feminine-but-certainly-always-fae glamour is the *encantado*. In Portuguese, it means the 'enchanted one'. (Such a name!) The encantado is an Amazonian river spirit who usually takes the form of the rare, pink dolphin: the *boto*. By day, boto live in the underwater realm of Encante. By night, they transform into handsome men and come ashore... particularly for parties and festivals. Always with a hat to conceal their cetacean blowhole. (Glamour requires the concealment of shortcomings!) These musicians would charm and seduce local women until the pre-dawn hours before returning to their watery home. They are forever drawn from their paradisiacal homes by the promise of human pleasure--fleeting and unreliable as it is.

There is wisdom in the story of the Encantado. Those rare moments, passing encounters, finding a lifelong best friend just for that one evening... They have an enduring value that is worthy of the pursuit of glamour.

Glamour, then, is an indwelling of the compelling and capricious. It is luck that you can wear. In my own life, I am lucky to have found Deb.

And now, so are you.
Gordon White
runesoup.com
London. 2013.

CHAPTER I

Getting Ready for a Complete Internal Aesthetic Change

Magic and Daily Life Improvements as a Gendered Concept

Firstly, it is my aim that people of all genders to feel comfortable using this book: Male, female, or your own gender identity that may be more fluid than either of those concepts. Women have been fighting for a very long time to be allowed to do the things that men do. It is by far not a perfect transition – I don't think I'll be calling myself "post-feminist" in this life time. While there are social (and sometimes even more serious repercussions) for women to do the things that men do – cut our hair short, wear jeans, smoke cigars, have seats in government positions, the armed forces -- in most first world countries these things are happening.

But are men doing the things that are considered more feminine? I think so. I think it's a slower process because there are less obvious benefits to being proficient in the female arts, though the benefits are there nonetheless.

Is magic a gendered concept? I think on its face it is. Low magic was once considered women's work while high magic was (mostly) something that only a man could do. Does some magic seem more masculine (Swords! Robes! Complicated chalkings!)Does some magic seem more feminine? (Herbs from the kitchen! Menstrual blood! Brooms!) I think it probably does. Does the concept of home improvement mean different things in context of gender? In the media, home improvement for a man means Home Depot, hammers, ladders and tools. For a woman it means Pottery Barn, throw pillows and duvet covers.

I think that if you want to be the fastest, brightest, and most cunning person in the twenty-first century, you need to be able to think outside what is stereotypically gendered. Women need to be able to do magic that comes from "boy world" and men need to be able to do magic from "girl world". I invite you to pick up a hammer and a nail to hang a picture if you have never done this. I invite you to select a bed set from sheets to bed skirt if this is a new experience. I invite you to use a blade in your ritual if you never have and I invite you to think of your kitchen herbs as more than spaghetti sauce. If any of my suggestions challenge you because they challenge your idea of who you are based on your gender, I invite you to give it a whirl! The worst that can happen is: It doesn't work for you. The *best* that can happen is: You have something shiny and new to use as part of your daily and magical arsenal.

What is Glamour?

One of the things that I find the most interesting about glamour is that it conjures a very specific image in people's heads. Because of that specific image, most people are then quick to either classify themselves as being glamorous or not being glamorous. What image do you have in your head when you think about the word *glamour*? Does it change if you're thinking about it from a magic context?

When I think of the word *glamour*, I think about old movies where the starlet is wearing diamonds, a satin dress, high heels, lipstick, and wavy hair. She's at a supper club and there's a band playing. Handsome men in white jackets are vying for her attention, all wanting to buy her champagne, or duck under glass. They're trying to get the next dance with her or matching wits with her while lighting her cigarette.

Do I look like this in my day-to-day life? Of course not! My day job is child care. My day-to-day life is spent hunched over a baby, a computer, or a spinning wheel. I need to wear clothes that can be machine washed. I'm often covered in tiny human bodily fluids and/or wool fiber. Glamour is something that gets overlooked in American society (a situation that would be frowned upon by the French and the Italians). Often, this even goes a step farther. If you are into glamour you are then often associated with being frivolous and vain. Many may even believe that you think you're better than everyone else. To which I say, "Whatever!"

Those are all tools to hold you back from being your most glamorous self. But, why is it important to be glamorous, to do magic? Think about it. Witches and other occultists were (and are) often perceived as glamorous because they're stepping outside the comfort of everyday life, just like you do when you do magic. Pop culture witches have worn anything from gothic school girl Lolita Chic (*The Craft*) to classic Little Black Dresses (*The Witches of Eastwick, Practical Magic*) to sexy seventies glam *(The Dunwich Horror)*.

Does being glamorous mean that you have to be something you're not? Does it mean you have to wear things that make you feel like you're in drag (and not in a good way)? Does it mean wearing ball gowns to work? No, of course not! The trick to being glamorous is figuring out who you are and how you want to present that to the world. Sharon Stone famously made a short sleeve turtle neck from the GAP famous in 1996 when she was presenting at the Oscars. Is a short sleeve turtle neck glamorous in and of itself? Not really. Can someone make it that way by the way she wears it? Definitely! If you think this is not true take another look at country singer Alan Jackson's torn blue jeans.

Let's delve a bit deeper. What does this have to do with magic? Well, if you want to be very specific and very precise, nothing really. I've done magic successfully in sweats at a messy, kitchen table with what I had in my kitchen cabinet. I've done magic successfully leading a Druidic ritual that took three months of planning and hundreds of dollars' worth of supplies.

But…

But. This book isn't about a numbers game—though magic can be. This is about looking more deeply into how you do magic and how you live your life. This is about bringing glamour back to ritual. Surface reasons? Because it's pretty. Because we eat with our eyes first. Because we live in a culture that undervalues beauty for beauty's sake and very narrowly defines what beauty is and what beauty is not.

Going a bit deeper with a simple daily life analogy: Your friends and loved ones love you for you. They know all your quirks, all the things that make you irritating, and all the ugly parts of you. They still love you anyway. They also see all the potential you have, everything that's good in you, all the kind deeds you do, and all the beauty you have inside you that makes you who you are. They love you when your house is messy and all you have to offer them is a warm beer and half a bag of Doritos. They love you when your house is sparkling and you have wine and fancy cheese to offer. But I do find that, when you put more effort into anything, it's appreciated more. Of course, your lover understands that you just worked a twelve-hour day on your feet. He or she isn't expecting a four-course meal when you get home. But, when you have time to rest, and when you are able, it's always appreciated when, instead of choosing to take that time to watch six hours of *The Real Housewives of Where Ever* in a coma-like state, eating spray cheese from the can, you instead chose to spend time doing something nice to show your lover that he is

10

appreciated. It creates an environment of reciprocity. (It was so nice you did something nice for me! When I'm able, I will do something nice for you!) This is not to be confused with an environment of *quid quo pro*. (I have done X for you so you will do Y for me.) Wouldn't it be the same with the gods and spirits? Wouldn't it be appreciated that you took the time, effort, and energy to create something beautiful for their enjoyment? Wouldn't that beauty spill over into your own everyday life and create a better environment for yourself by doing so? Those are trick questions. I've been working on this for some time now and I can tell you the answer is: Yes!

So what does glamour mean in magic? Well, in movies, books, and legends it was about being able to do crazy things like change your appearance completely, disappear, or even fly. In this modern life though? It means something much more important. Glamour is the ability to literally be *charming*. For people to be *charmed* by you.

Webster's Dictionary defines charming as: *extremely pleasing or delightful:* entrancing *<a charming restaurant>*. Well I don't know about you, but I find it extremely helpful for both myself and others to find me very *pleasing* or *delightful*. It has helped me be able to love the skin I'm in. It has helped me get the career I want. It has helped me make sales. It has helped me find the right romantic partners for myself, and it's helped me be able to be in the right place at the right time so that things will occasionally fall into my lap. Very simply, it makes my life easier.

And isn't that what magic is for?

Throughout this book, I will be discussing glamour through many different lenses.

We will discuss glamour:

- In your everyday, non-ritual life. We will discuss bringing glamour to your ritual life.
- In a specific ritual format that I've developed to bring more glamour, in all its aspects, into your life.
- In context of working with specific spirits that can assist you to bring glamour into your life.
- With specific spell work you can utilize in your practice to bring more *dolce vita* into your world.

But before we get into all of that, I find many people have roadblocks internally against glamour. I think it's important to spend some time unpacking that baggage before getting into the nuts and bolts of glamour work. Here are some questions to consider—and, ideally, resolve—before moving forward.

1. Do you consider yourself a glamorous person? Why or why not?

2. Think about two people you find glamorous, one famous and one whom you know in "real" life. How do you feel about those people? If you find yourself feeling emotions such as bitterness, anger, or envy, why do you feel that way?

3. Did anyone in your life tell you that you *had* to look a

certain way? How did that affect you? How does that affect you now?

4. Do you find being glamorous a gendered idea? If so, is it part of a gender construct outside you?

5. Does the idea of glamour make you feel not good enough or excluded? If so, why?

6. Do you feel you need to be rich to be glamorous? If so, why?

7. Do you feel that your socio-economic background and/or education and/or upbringing prevent you from being glamorous? If so, why?

8. Does your relationship with your body keep you from being glamorous? If so, why?

9. What do you find glamorous about yourself?

10. What do you have in your wardrobe right now that makes you feel glamorous?

11. What compliment have you received in your life that has made you feel glamorous?

12. What is your most *glamorous* experience in life?

13. What areas in your life could you use *glamour* based magic to improve it?

Once you find the answers to these questions for yourself, you'll have a much better idea about where your areas of comfort and where your areas of discomfort are when dealing with the idea of glamour. These answers will give you a really good starting point in your journey to bring more glamour into your life.

CHAPTER II

The Arte of Glamour

Although it may not seem like it on the surface, this book is being built in a deliberate manner. The changes I'm asking you to make in your daily life are to prepare you for the ritual work I will be establishing later in the book. Small, every-day changes are much harder to make a habit and a routine than significant ones. An ecstatic ritual experience feels so much bigger, so much more important. This is why it's so much easier to have ritual work as an isolated incident as opposed to it being the ground work for real change in your life. The daily work is the cake. The ritual work is the fondant with amazing designs that you layer on the top of the cake. Neither is as awesome without the other.

Your ritual work and daily work can achieve a certain synchronicity to help you establish the life you want to be leading on a spiritual, professional, emotional, and intellectual level. Start by clarifying, to yourself, what you want to accomplish in bringing more glamour into your life. Ask yourself the following questions:

1. **What's my hook? How would I like to describe my life?**
    A hook is something that can be explained in one short sentence. For example: When trying to make the movie *Speed* it was described as "*Die Hard* on a bus." I describe my blog as: "Radical Practicality".

2. **How do I want people to see me? What do I want people to think about me, based on my appearance at a first meeting? How do I want to be perceived professionally? How do I want to be perceived by friends? How do I want to be perceived by family? How do I want to be perceived by lovers, potential or current?**

3. **How do I want to see myself professionally, intellectually, emotionally, socially, and spiritually?**

4. **What do I want my spiritual practice to look like?**

5. **What do I want my home to look like?**

6. **What are my goals: professionally, intellectually, emotionally, socially, and spiritually?**

You're going to fail at being equally good at all spheres at all times. This is the part in memoirs and life improvement books that I gloss over. Surely I will be able to achieve perfection unlike every other human being on this entire planet?

Let me repeat. **You are going to fail at being equally good at all spheres at all times.** *Do not gloss over this.* You are going to miss critical opportunities presented to you by the Universe, your gods, your spirits, and flesh-and-blood people in your life if you get all caught up in an OCD loop about wanting to be perfect. Trust me. If you are a perfectionist, you are going to screw yourself over if you get caught up in the quest for perfection over the quest for leading the life you want to be leading. Which do you think is more critical: Spending an hour trying to find the perfect synonym for a word or spending an hour writing a first draft?

If you find yourself getting caught up in a perfectionist loop, the best thing to do is to fail on purpose. This is like liquid burning in the eyes to perfectionists. But, you need to. Burn an egg. Spill something on the carpet on purpose. Leave the house with mismatched socks. (Nothing cute and fun! I'm talking a navy and a black.) Most of all, give yourself some space to fail creatively. Some of my ugliest dyeing experiments have resulted in the most gorgeous handspun yarn. Buy a canvas and some paints—especially if you're not a fine artist—and just let yourself experiment. Make something for dinner you think you'll hate. *Failing is critical to succeeding.* Make sure you have that under control before you go forward.

If you do everything I have suggested to do in this book, you are going to completely shake up your internal ant farm. Tunnels will collapse. Not every ant farm occupant will survive. New routes will have to be designed. Escape from the ant farm itself is possible.

Here is where I ask you: Before you start the spiritual aspect, are you really prepared for change? ***Do not gloss over this*** *aspect.* Change is terrifying. If you're really working on changing your life completely, fear and despair are going to be your constant companions. This isn't a publisher-paid excursion around the world where you get to explore your culinary palate, your meditational practice, and find love in Bali a la *Eat, Pray, Love* (which I love as a book, by the way). This is you intentionally fucking up situations while your regular life goes on. You don't get to escape to some nice place you've never been and journal thoughtfully about your experiences. You still have bills to pay. You still have a job or a need to look for one. You still have your regular spiritual practice. You still have friends, family and lovers. You still have a boss. You still have to make dinner. You still have all the problems you had before.

This is way more *Cleaving* than *The Julie/Julia Project.* (Hint: If you haven't read both books by Julie Powell, *The Julie/Julia Project* is a whimsical romp depicting Powell cooking her way through Julia Child's *Mastering the Art of French Cooking. Cleaving* is about the affairs that Powell had, her deteriorating marriage, her problems with addictive substances, and how she learns to become a butcher.)

You don't go on this journey in a vacuum. Do you have a good support structure? You'll need one. If you do already, it would be awfully polite to check in with them to make sure that they're willing to support you while you go on this jaunt through reorganizing your entire internal curio cabinet. Sometimes, marriages and relationships break during a time like this. The reasons for that are twofold: the explorer failed to check in with her spouse/significant other *before* starting the journey to give the spouse/significant other a chance to ask questions, raise objections and give input as well as co-signing onto the exploration full-heartedly so that the spouse/significant other can be a full partner in this adventure or the exploration smashes open cracks in the relationship past repair.

A good relationship can withstand internal change if you communicate with your partner about what you are trying to achieve and why. A good relationship expects change. But it also has to be change in a direction that you and your partner have agreed on. If you suddenly decide you want to live in Alaska—no matter what—and want to uproot your family who has connections, familial ties, and outstanding career opportunities in New York and you agreed to live in New York for life, this is going to be poorly received—especially if it's given as an order. Your complete internal change does not give you carte blanche to act like a jerk to everyone else in your life. Compromises can be made on both sides if your personal exploration is presented correctly (i.e., as a team sport). Share the answers to the questions listed above. Have good, thoughtful conversations about how these changes will potentially change things. Discuss if you're going on this journey together or on your own with support. Discuss how things such as household work need to be renegotiated.

It's good to talk with family members like parents, siblings as well as close friends about these changes. There's a big difference between: "She won't return my calls and she's a self-absorbed asshat!" and: "I understand that the projects you're working on take up a lot of your time so let's be sure to schedule time so that I don't feel neglected and you can accomplish what you're trying to accomplish."

Despite doing what you need to do to inform people close to you about what you are trying to accomplish, it may feel ethereal to others, especially if you don't live together. If you are doing your best to compromise but they want more than you can feasibly give, you need to decide where to hold your lines. I find a simple: "I can't do x with you on y date because I'm working as I have told you. I'm free on z dates. Do you want to get together on one of those dates?" works because it can be a polite but boundary-policing broken record phrase.

You may wonder why I'm not telling you to accomplish whatever you're trying to accomplish no matter what. People close to you, be damned! Well that answer is simple: It's because you're going to be a complete wreck some days. You're going to need people to hold you up when you have days when you can't stop crying at work and dinner feels like an impossible feat that is far beyond your comprehension and you're wondering why you've decided to torture yourself by wanting to achieve difficult goals and self-change instead of sticking to the status quo where everything is safe and warm and comfortable. You need people who will read your writing, read your cover letters, go to the post office to ship for you, make dinner, pick up the slack at home, help you brain storm, let you verbally throw up all over them and tell you that they still love you and believe in you. If you're doing this journey correctly, emotional stability has just become an abstract concept and there is no normal.

Without support, making huge changes for yourself is almost impossible because, again, your daily life doesn't stop. You don't get to montage out the days where you're almost throwing up on yourself because you can't pay your bills. You don't get to gloss over the nine sleepless nights in a row where you spend the evening staring at the ceiling wondering why you're doing this to yourself. You don't get to speed past the fights you're going to have with your loved ones because you're a stressed out artiste/maniac to live with. You're not at a point where you can laugh about how you used to live with fear and despair on a daily basis but now everything is cheese and daisies. You're still living in the hard part. The hard part is where most people quit and retreat back to their safe cozy places that their lizard brains approve.

If you want to push past the hard part, you need to live in the moment and all the hard parts it brings with it. You need to be surrounded by people who are willing to help hold you up during this time. I can't tell you how much I've cried huge heaving, completely-humiliating-at-two-in-the-afternoon sobs to my mom. She's minding her own business in her work place where I stress her out like whoa and need to be talked down. Every time she says: *Just give it a little longer. Just give it a little longer. Take a deep breath and have a glass of wine when you get home. Relax. You can do this.*

My husband-elect, Jow, has done more post office runs, craft finishing, and cooked more dinners than anyone who works six days a week has any business doing. Gordon has answered more of my insecure, completely neurotic emails with sound, practical advice than anyone an ocean away should be responsible for. The list goes on. Without my supporters, I couldn't do this. They help me find the parts of me that are brave. You need that. Take the time to figure out what you're trying to do and the support structure you'll need to do it before you go any farther.

CHAPTER III

The Arte of Vous

Make over montage! It's my favorite part of every girlie girl movie I've ever watched. My favorite make over montage ever was from *St. Trinian's* which was based on the comics from the fifties about a group of school girls getting into all kinds of mischief. But what I liked best was that when Annabelle got her make overs from all the different cliques in the school, at the end of the day, she chose the look that she felt was most her. She didn't feel pressured into just getting in line with the popular girls. She took a little bit from everyone and made her own look, one that worked for her.

Let me be clear: I am not interested in forcing you to be anything you're not. I am not interested in forcing you into any kind of gender construct you are not comfortable with. I am not interested in making you be something you're not. You know why? Because it won't stick. You'll be like a toddler wriggling out of an outfit she doesn't want to be wearing and streaking across the country club in fifteen minutes flat. When I got my first grown up job, my mom took me shopping for all kinds of suits from Macys in a variety of crazy colors. There were scarves involved and non-natural fabrics. I felt like a little girl pretending to be my mom—only I had to do it for eight hours a day, five days a week. I felt miserable and I didn't know what to do about it.

But if I didn't dress like a grown up, how was I going to be taken seriously and get promoted and run the company by thirty? I soon realized that other things were hindering my desired rate of rapid promotion. I needed to learn how to, like, interact in an office environment. I needed to learn how to fix the stupid copy machine no matter what crap it pulled, and I needed to learn to be super pro-active. This made me lose all desire to actually get anywhere in the company. I decided to just be me (within reason) and clock in my three years, do my job the way they wanted, and then get out immediately. Being me meant that I decorated my cube with iridescent fabrics, put up pictures of goddesses, listened to NIN at a low volume. I was dressed appropriately for the workplace. Sort of. I was dressed like me but within the guidelines of my company. I wore circle skirts with sweater sets and pearls, and clompy boots with sparkly laces. I got promoted and would have kept getting promoted if I hadn't had enough of corporate America and decided to get out and go back to jobs that are better suited to introverts with low people interaction and low expectation of playing "the game". I can play "the game" just fine! But, I get annoyed by it and would rather just do my job.

My point is that I want to make you the best you that you can be. This involves looking at you holistically including: your appearance, your dwellings, and your magical practice to your spirit. When you are your "best you" it's a lot easier to make magic happen. More importantly, it's a lot easier to enjoy the process. I ask that you try the whole process before discarding bits. If you are like me, you'll discard that last sentence and do what you want anyway. But, honestly, take it from a chick who distains reading the manual and never wants to follow the rules! I think you'll get the most out of this by going through the entire process from start to finish. *I've* gotten the most out of doing it that way–and I'm really stubborn!

Your Home

Anyone who has ever read my blog, my articles, or my eCourse knows that I'm a fanatic about having a clean house—as much as possible. This would make my mother laugh until we had to have her committed because I was a slovenly child and teen and, as an *artiste,* I still tend towards disorder if left to my own devices. As Jow points out, I'm not yet to a point where I have my own brick and mortar store or storage space and I also don't yet have a workshop outside of the home. This means that my condo (which is less than 1,000 square feet) is my living space and my creating space. It also means that, at times, my condo looks like Candy Spelling's wrapping room vomited all over the condo.

I don't expect you to be Miss Martha. I am not Miss Martha. If you saw my house for the last month where I've been sick and crafting, you would not be impressed. You will not be able to exert order over your living space at all times especially if you are ever ill, work too much, have children and/or have slovenly housemates. Everything does not need to look like a Container Store clean room. But if we're discussing the philosophy of æsthetics in a modern context, we need to discuss your living space.

Firstly, have you really and truly moved into your living space? It's going to be more difficult to establish a base of power/hearth space if you still have your stuff in boxes and you've never gotten around to hanging pictures or curtains or whatever makes you feel established within a living space. You need to establish this space as *yours*. Even if you're renting. Especially if you're renting. You can still decorate, bring in fresh flowers, and hang curtains if you're renting. I would know! I rented for way longer than I ever owned.

Every house tends to have areas that are reasonably neat and areas that are bluntly a complete clusterfuck. It's not a charming arrangement of materials you're working with. It's just a mess. You know in your heart what the difference is. Figure out where your mess lurks and start de-cluttering it. Generally the areas that need to be de-cluttered tend to be closets, junk drawers, laundry rooms, bedrooms. In short: Any area that company does not see. Think about how to better reorganize the problem areas. If this isn't your area of expertise, then either get a copy of *Real Simple* magazine which specializes in this kind of thing or consult your neat freak friend/family member. We all have one.

A key point in de-cluttering is getting rid of things you no longer need. This is an area of difficulty for most people. "No longer need" can be hard to define. For me, getting rid of things I didn't need became easier when I was going through my divorce. I was renting a town home and my ex-husband had decided it would be awesome for him to just take the things he wanted and to leave about fifty contractors' bags of his junk for me to clean up after him. Since I was tossing so much anyway, and I was moving without the help of movers, it was a lot easier for me to become less attached to a lot of my stuff.

There are things that everyone's attached to. For me, it's the first notebook I ever wrote my first story in, photos, and clothing. Photos and some periodicals aren't a big deal for my storage space. Most of my pictures are electronic at this point anyway. But I tend to attach a lot of sentimental attachment to my wardrobe. So, it's harder for me to weed them out. Wardrobe is also something that needs to be weeded out more frequently. Questions that I ask myself when trying to figure out whether to keep or toss include: *Have I worn this less than a year ago? Is it something that's irreplaceable? Do I have any pictures of me wearing this? Am I keeping it in the hopes that I'll wear it again "someday"? Is there anything I can do with it if I'm not wearing it? Is it taking up a lot of space?* It's also important to remember when trying to de-clutter that you can take a picture of an item so you still have it that way and that even if you donate something, if it was important to you, you still have the memory from that item. Most of the time it's not about the corset itself (in my case). It's the memories of my wild maidenhood that I have associated with it. I'm afraid if I get rid of the corset, I'll lose the memories. I've sold off a few corsets that I know I have very little hope of fitting into again and frankly I don't go to too many Goth events anymore. Did I lose the memories associated with those corsets? Nope. And when I'm with the right friends, we take out some pictures and reminisce.

When de-cluttering, be sure to see what's in shape to donate and what's seen better days. Before donating, make sure that the place you have in mind takes the kinds of items you want to donate. I find, in New Jersey, that donating books is actually a very difficult endeavor. I found that the Lupus Foundation took everything I needed to donate which included: books, clothes, and small appliances. Of course, there's always the option to sell things on Amazon or eBay as well as having a garage sale.

Now that you've de-cluttered, it's time to make sure everything's physically clean. If this is a very daunting process for you, it may be worth getting a one-time professional house cleaning service to get things in good shape so that you can maintain it. If you would like to embark on this adventure yourself, but don't know where to start, you may want to subscribe to Flylady.net. This site offers free strategies for house cleaning.

What does all this de-cluttering and house cleaning have to do with magic? I have honestly found that the energy flows much better in our home when things are de-cluttered. It makes doing magic a lot easier if everything's flowing well already. Magic can still, of course, happen in a messy house. But, it's the difference between taking a shower with a clogged drain and a clean drain. You're getting clean in both scenarios. A clean drain is just less of a hassle.

Now that you've cleaned and de-cluttered, you can now work on getting your house magically cleansed. I've magically cleansed when my house was a mess, hoping that it would help get the energy moving better. But, it's sort of like adding a teabag to a cup of cold water. It doesn't do much. (Regrettably!) Feel free to come up with your own cleansing process. In case you don't have one, here's mine:

1. I keep a straw broom (Bought from Michaels. Mine's undecorated. But, if your inner Martha wants to get out the glue gun, go crazy!) I have it over my front door. It's magically charged to cleanse space and blessed with Florida Water to keep that banishing energy going. When I am not using the broom, I have it fixed up to the door firmly enough that you can open and shut the door without knocking the broom down, but not so firmly that it can't fall. I know if the broom falls, trouble's coming. I

use the broom to sweep out each room of the house including sweeping closets and mirrors. Then, I sweep all that negative energy out of my front door. You need to take it outside or it's like having a monster negative energy dust bunny sitting on the middle of your living room floor.

2. I open as many windows and doors as seasonally possible (even if it's just a crack) to air out the house.

3. I sage each of the rooms (closets and mirrors too) to get the sluggish and/or negative energy moving.

4. If I have been particularly slovenly about keeping up with my magical house cleansing, I may do a pass through the house with the House Cleansing incense that I make. You can make your own or buy mine at The Glamoury Apothecary on Etsy if you feel you need to take this step.

5. I keep a salt bowl in the center of my house. It's a ceramic bowl with a black glass skull in it. Mr. Skull works with the salt to eat up negative crap that other

people bring into my home. He requires a salt change when I do a magical cleansing. He's very particular (with me at least. If you get a Mr. Skull, yours may be different!) about how I do it. All salt in the bowl must be washed down the drain. Then the bowl and the skull must be dried off. Mr. Skull likes a thin layer of black salt (preferably fancy black salt from William Sonoma) for him to perch on top of. Then, he likes to be completely covered with coarse kosher or sea salt so he can hide. You don't need a skull in your bowl. But having a spirit devoted to assisting you in cleaning negative energy is as useful as a couple of sucker fish who like to eat algae in an aquarium. It just makes your life easier. Awakening a small spirit like Mr. Skull is a process very similar to awakening a Mojo Hand's spirit. (I will cover this a bit later in the book if you need help with that aspect.) If you chose to not use a Mr. Skull of your own, a bowl with salt alone still helps.

6. Feeding time at the zoo! I feed my Mojo Hands, my Honey Pot, my Desert Roses, my lodestones and my High John root which all work on bringing me money.

7. Now everything is very clean. So, it's a good time for me to make offerings to my gods and spirits. I offer tea lights and water to everyone.

Drag

RuPaul once said that you're born naked and everything else is just drag. Appearance tends to be a touchy subject in the magical community. I think it's because many of us have some discomfort with our "meat suits". Maybe we don't feel they're accurate representations of what we feel really lives inside of us. Perhaps we tend to be societal edge dwellers as it is and we don't like The Man (or occult book writers) to tell us what to do.

Here's the thing. You can absolutely be yourself and still "dress for success". I'm defining success as *you* feeling successful about *you* in *your* endeavors not some nebulous billionaire image with all the accoutrements that society tells you you're supposed to have. Does this mean that you don't have to dress like your boss to get ahead? Yes. Does it mean you don't have to wear a suit to a wedding or a funeral? No. Let's start unpacking all of that, shall we?

If I dressed like my last boss (whom I loved best) to get

ahead, I'd look ridiculous. My boss was a fashionable lady who was also about thirty years my senior. We're getting back into "mom clothes" territory again with that. While my boss did take some time to play *Dress Me up Corporate Barbie* with me before our company folded, she was smart enough to take me to a place that had a personal shopper who was approximately my age and had roughly my budget. Jamie scoured the sales racks to find clothes that I could afford and that were "youthful". (That's code for: *older than a twenty-year-old, younger than a fifty-year-old.*)

I think dressing like your boss is sort of an antiquated notion that is meant for young men in 1980's corporate America because suits were less an issue of age appropriateness. Now, most people don't wear suits every day in the workplace. It can be harder to tell a Ralph Lauren that was bought on super discount at Macy's and a Ralph Lauren that was custom-made for you—unless you're a serious clothing dork like I am. Most people aren't and will not know the difference.

So, am I saying you don't have to follow rules? Let's not get crazy. Certain rules exist for a reason. For example, there is a rational for what to wear to an important social function such as a wedding or a funeral or important career-related functions such as a job interview. These occasions require specific attire so that you show respect. You show the part of you that is socially mandated and so you don't make an ass of yourself in front of people you either care about or respect. You can still be you! Your guidelines are just much tighter. Frankly, as a grown ass adult, I think you can handle having to kowtow to other people's wishes for what is likely no more than twenty days of the entire year. If you find yourself feeling in drag in a bad way that is distressing to you for more time than that, then it's time for you to re-evaluate some of the life decisions that have put you in that position.

So what do you need to accommodate standard expectations on special occasions? A dark-colored suit in the gender of your choosing with conservative lines will get you through job interviews and funerals. A little black dress or a more festively colored suit will get you through the weddings. Keep them for only those occasions. Have them hung up in your closet, dry cleaned regularly, and tailored or repaired as needed. If you do that, they will last a lot longer.

When selecting this attire, choose something that is well made with good fabric. (This does not necessarily mean more expensive.) Select something that has a "timeless" look (such as a sheath dress or a pinstripe suit), something that fits well, and something that doesn't make you feel like an uncomfortable toddler. If you're making a face in the mirror as soon as you put it on in the dressing room, move on to other options. You may not find something that you love and that feels like it's intrinsically you. However, you can find something you feel at the very least neutral towards. As always, if you don't like skirts or paisley, don't buy skirts or paisley! How can you make it feel more you? Color choice, fabric choice, and choice in accessories (shoes, jewelry, handbags, belt, wallet, even underwear) can do a lot to make a garment feel more comfortable.

So now that we've covered the aspect that's that touchiest, let's get to the fun part: Your everyday wear. A good starting place with this is to ask yourself the following questions:

What image am I trying to express to the world? What is my favorite thing in my wardrobe and why? Who do I know that I admire with their fashion choices?

I think you can be fashionable and still be *you,* regardless of your age, job function, and budget. For me, getting past the big 3-0 was hard. I had to do some serious wardrobe re-evaluation. My weight had changed. My career had changed, and my social life had changed. It took me a while to get my wardrobe to change accordingly. I realized I needed clothes that reflected my current life, not my past life. For me, that meant fashionable, washable clothes that could be vomited on for my day job as a nanny, weekend clothes where I wanted to be cute and comfortable, date night clothes for a standard midweek day, and party clothes for going to a bar or a party.

The nanny part was probably the hardest for me. Whatever I chose to wear on the job couldn't be anything I was ridiculously attached to. There was always the chance that baby fluids would make the garment unsalvageable. At the same time, past a certain point, I couldn't just buy yoga pants from Old Navy because I had to replace them every three months. This was becoming a cost sink for me. I also didn't want to sport the "new mom" look wherein I look like I haven't slept in weeks, will never sleep in weeks, and have possibly lost my will to live.

My fashionable mommy friend, Jenn, helped me pull my day look together through her Pinterest board. I learned that The Gap had a mail order company called Athleta that I never knew existed. They specialize in fashionable workout clothing that wears well, works in urban surroundings as well as rock climbing in some remote place, and is super comfortable. It was a lot more than I had been spending on yoga pants. Nevertheless, for me, having them make my butt look great and having no fabric pilling or fading made it a very worth the extra cost. Athleta also introduced me to concepts like mini-skirts with attached Capri leggings underneath them –which I love. I also learned that tee shirts made from pima cotton were a worthwhile investment. The fabric holds up so much better than a poly blend and the colors don't fade as easily.

Style Overhaul Checklist:

- Anything that you have not worn in a year or more should be donated unless there is an exceptional sentimental attachment.

- Figure out what kinds of clothes you need for your lifestyle. What do you need to be stylish for work? For going out? For the weekend? For sleepwear? What wardrobe basics do you need for your lifestyle and climate region? Playing with a board on Pinterest could help you figure out what you're trying to accomplish. In my fantasy shopping world, I have a ton of 1950's "cupcake" garden party dresses and skirts. In reality land, I have to haul merchandise in boxes for my crafting. I have two cats that shed. I nanny for two very small children, and I don't go to formal cocktail parties very often at all. Does that mean I can't own any dresses/skirts like that? Of course not! But should my wardrobe have a lot of them? Probably not. Figuring out how to be glamorous in your every-day life can be challenging. But, it shouldn't involve anything but you being the best *you* that you can be.

- You shouldn't buy things that are beyond your budget. It defeats the purpose of being the best *you* if you have to go into massive debt to do so. However, you should buy the best that you can afford. Does that mean you can't have nice things? Of course not! If you want to shop some place that's *just* out of your budget, your best bet is to get on their eList so that they email you when they're having massive sales that bring some of their items into your budget range. It's also a good idea to figure out what's worth spending money on and what's not. Bottoms (yoga pants, athletic skirts…) are worth the investment for me. I want my tee shirts to be 100% cotton, preferably pima but I can accomplish that at the Gap on sale for $10. I don't need to go to Neiman Marcus for tee shirts the babies are going to poop on.

- Is there someone in your life that has a style similar to what you are trying to accomplish with a similar budget? Ask him or her for help shopping. If not, that's okay, too. Figure out what stores are in your price range and have the kind of clothes you like to wear. Then ask a friendly-looking salesperson for help. First off, it's their job. Second, having worked in retail, I know that the day can be super boring and slow if all you're doing is restocking shelves. Playing dress up with a stranger is much more fun for everyone. In order to really have the salesperson's attention, go during the week and make sure it's not a half hour before closing. If your budget is a little more high-end, stores like Bloomingdales, Joseph A. Banks, and Anthropologie specialize in offering free personal shopping services. This is really helpful if you have a difficult size because everything is pulled for you instead of you getting discouraged at the racks. Also ,if you have a difficult size, check store websites. Often, their online inventory will offer a much more extended selection of sizes online and will ship for free if you spend x amount of money. Then you can have your own personal dress up party session in the comfort of your own bathroom and can either mail back the items you don't like (for free) or return them in store.

- Accessorizing is where you can really show your own personal style. It is also what really pulls an outfit together. Make sure to save a little money for that. Things like purses and shoes are good investment pieces because, unless you get something crazy, they're pretty timeless. A corset looks even more impressive with a gorgeous necklace and a suit coat looks snazzier with a stylish watch (even if we don't use watches much anymore!). Other accessories include: rings, bracelets, earrings, coordinated socks and scarves.

- What is your skin care regime like? You definitely want to make sure you're using the right facial cleanser for your skin type as well as a moisturizer (which often contains sunscreen) and possibly other products depending on your skin type. It's a good idea to talk to a professional about this. Many CVS pharmacies have beauty advisors as do specialty stores like Lush.

- Good foundation garments are critical, as well, for both genders. If you feel good about your under things, it's easier to feel good about your outer wear as well! Pick out styles that make you feel attractive and that support your respective "bits" well. If you wear a bra, make sure you get measured yearly by someone who knows what she's doing because your size changes all the times. Toss out anything older than a couple years–even if it's in good repair. Elastic wears out by then and even with regular washings, it's the best thing to do for hygiene purposes.

- If you are inclined to wear makeup, figure out what you're hoping to accomplish. Do you want to look more dramatic or natural? Go to a store like Sephora or Ulta where they have beauty advisors and many brands (and budgets) to choose from.

Describe what you're looking for.

La Dolce Vita

Basically, any culture that doesn't have direct geographical ties to the Mediterranean has a hard time enjoying life. And with good reason. You're either living in abject poverty and/or you're in a culture that has a harsh climate and/or harsh political views and/or you're in a culture that values career/backbreaking labor over everything else. This does not make for party people. On the other hand, the French and the Italians (among others) are laissez-faire Catholics who like to eat well, dress well, work enough to pay bills, and bone their spouses. Most people in those cultures could give a crap less about "getting ahead"! They don't have five-year plans and long-term goals. They don't have all the cultural edicts that make it so that I have trouble sleeping at night.

My best friend, April, and I like to go back and forth about this. She thinks that there's no hope for us to ever have any kind of French confidence. She is convinced that French women are universally hated (even by each other) because they were born to think they are the cat's pajamas even if they have no empirical data to back it up! Conversely, we've been seeped in a pot of eating disorders and a variety of media telling everyone that no one is good enough. We've been raised in a society that has no regard for personal quality of life.

41

April does make valid points (and was *thrilled* to meet fat French women in Disneyworld). It is really hard to replicate a culture in a country that expects you to work 40+ hours a week, prices fast food cheaper than salads, and requires a car to get everywhere. I did learn a lot during my year's experiment. A key point is to stop thinking in terms of international business culture. (*Time is money!*) Start thinking more like Mediterranean culture. (*Time is not money; time is your life!*)

Really think about that phrase for a bit. It's true, honestly. Time *is* your life. How do you want to spend it? Well, I still want to write my book, get my business off the ground, and earn an income through my day job. It's not like I had this revelation to stop putting my shoulder to the wheel in a typical American fashion and now I magically can live life like a Mediterranean culture where I have a three-hour mid-day nap because it's Wednesday.

But I think it's important to live life more deeply. Business-motivated cultures (like the US, the UK, and Japan,) don't value living life more deeply that because it can't be quantified. It goes more deeply than you would think.

In previous relationships, I have been accused of being a gold digger because those exes could definitively state that they put x amount of cash into our relationship/me. Since I opted to primarily swan around doing "unimportant" things like feeding these exes, doing their shopping, listening to their problems, taking care of administrative tasks like paying bills, making our house a home, keeping house, paying my share of the bills, and making them gifts with my own two little hands, nothing I contributed to the relationship mattered.

Their ROI wasn't what *they* wanted so *I* didn't count. That's a terrible head trip. It's the logical progression of where our culture takes us that scorned exes feel cheated and can talk shit about you to others because they were able to put a price tag on your relationship and you were not.

So, let's step away from that toxic place. Instead, let's figure out ways to be able to live in a business-driven culture and still accomplish the things we want to accomplish. Further, let's do this while being able to at least have an *amuse bouche* of Mediterranean culture to help us keep us balanced.

Food is a really good starting place. Do you get enough fresh food in your diet? Not only does it help you to be more healthy, but also we really eat with our eyes first. Too much fast food, high carb, and high sugar food can make us feel sluggish and unmotivated. It honestly messes with me on an energetic level. It's harder for me to do magic when eating a lot of junk because my energy isn't flowing correctly which in turn makes me feel too lazy to be bothered to do any kind of spell work or ritual. I'm not saying you need to be on a diet or eat perfectly nutritious meals at all times. But making some small changes to your diet in order to eat better can give you more energy to accomplish the things you want to accomplish.

It's much more than that! I know I tend to eat in front of the television and/or computer. I'm not paying attention to what I'm shoveling into my maw and I'm not really taking the time to enjoy it. If that's the case, why bother trying to eat enjoyable things at all if I don't even notice what I'm eating? Just the act of being present while eating a meal can really change what the meal does for you. Eating dinner at least whenever possible without media interruptions is a good way to connect with the people you live with or just to have some quality time with yourself. It's time you can spend reflecting on your day. Cooking for yourself and others is another good check to see if you're living life as fully as possible. It doesn't have to be something crazily complicated. I certainly count getting olives, cheese, a dried meat, and fresh bread as *cooking*. Making meals like that gives you the chance to really enjoy the process of procuring the goods (smelling, looking, touching, tasting—when permitted—and even listening to your local grocer). It makes the process of doing a mundane task so much richer. Taking time to arrange these items on a plate and sitting down and eating without media interruption slows down time to a Mediterranean pace, if only for a half an hour. (Okay, fifteen or twenty minutes!) Even if you do nothing but talk about television and the blogosphere, it's still a different experience from watching television, texting, and blogging. (Not that I would know anything about that!)

Movement is another key factor in our lives that Americans especially do not excel at. Most of us outside of NYC don't rely on public transportation and walking to get places. This is a really big problem. It's not good for our hearts and it's not good for our stress levels. Jow and I have figured out that it takes us approximately twenty minutes to walk from our house to my mom's house and back. We need to do that loop as often as possible for a few reasons: One, it gives us uninterrupted time together to decompress about our respective days. Two, walking tends to make my brain work better so I can think more clearly about whatever is bugging me or how to accomplish whatever never-ending to-do-list task I have to complete. Three, it helps me make sure my heart doesn't stop. You would think these would be ample reasons to be *religious* about the walk. Right? Nope. My monkey mind hates it! It insists that walking will be boring, hot (or cold depending on the season) and my time would be much better spent lying on the couch watching *Gossip Girl* rather than connecting with my husband-elect. It's so bad that if I step foot into our cozy little condo there is no chance my fat ass is walking anywhere. So I have to outsmart my own laziness. I make sure I have walking shoes in my car, that I wear clothes I can walk in, and that I wait for Jow to come home in my car, texting or surfing on my phone in my own home parking space like a psycho. But it works! There's not enough time for me to get comfortable with being a slag in my home. So, we walk. I'm not a great walker. I have weak ankles. I'm fat, and I have fibromyalgia. My pace could generously be described as plodding. But it's so good for me and makes me feel so much better about life in general. Not to mention that I need to be able to fulfill basic human functions: walking, sleeping, eating, toileting, breathing/not choking on my own spit… in order to feel like I have some modicum of dignity.

The third important aspect of infusing some Mediterranean living into your life is sensuality. There's the obvious: having good sex which can make many people feel better about their lot in life—even if it's self-directed, shall we say. But perhaps sex isn't your thing or you don't have a partner/don't enjoy self-directed solo activity. Well, sex is really the tip of the iceberg in sensual living. *Sensual* really doesn't even mean sex per se. It's about living fully through your senses. Having a nice environment to live in fulfills your sense of sight. Having your environment smell a way that you enjoy fulfills your sense of smell. Wearing clothes that feel nice on you fulfills your sense of touch. Listening to music that really moves you fulfills your sense of hearing. Eating one piece of really decadent chocolate fulfills your sense of taste. Sensuality is all about taking pleasure in the minor and the mundane because that's where you need it most. If you can't savor those small moments in your life, it doesn't help you. You become a stressed-out wreck of a human being.

I like spinning yarn because touching all of those different kinds of fiber is a really sensual experience for me. I love going to my favorite grocery store and having the deli person give me a taste of a new meat. I love listening to Lana del Ray's *Born to Die* album in my car. I love her voice and her lyrics. Listening to her makes me feel like I'm a girl who was born in too much privilege, who likes to drink Cristal, and run around with bad boys. I like a bra that doesn't have nine thousand hooks and isn't padded from here to kingdom come because it makes me feel sexy. I like really rich and glittery lipstick and eye shadow palettes from Sephora. I like arranging small grocery store flowers into teacups in my house while burning incense bought at my local Indian cash and carry. It's vital to have small pleasures that you can enjoy for yourself on a daily basis. Without them, life gets to feeling too heavy, too stressful, and pointless.

Ennui, as sexy as it is in theory, in practice just makes you sluggish. Sluggishness makes it hard for you to do magic effectively. The more places you are already succeeding in life, the easier it is to give your life a little magical push and to be succeeding in the places in which you find yourself lagging.

I am not one of those girls for whom all this comes easy. I wear my hair in a ponytail, if left to my own devices. My makeup technique before lots and lots of instruction was recently gently described as "previously train wreck-like" by a dear friend. My mom wouldn't even help me organize my house until the last three years because my house keeping was lacking too much to even start. I used to shotgun McDonald's Snack Wraps while drinking a ton of Triple XXX Vitamin Water and eat Cheeseburger Big Bites from the 7-11, drunk on rotgut tequila as primary food sources. Most of my furniture still comes from Ikea. Without a lot of self-work, I tend to spend my downtime curled in an immobile ball on my Ikea couch eating a whole bag of Chex Mix with a Crumbs giant cupcake shooter while watching six hours straight of *Intervention* with rapt, anxious attention.

I'm a nervous, shaky animal who gets socially flustered super easily. I'm telling you all this because my whole theory is *great Goddess above! If I can just pull myself together, I might actually live up to the image of someone who some people want to emulate.* (It is frankly terrifying to me that people would want to emulate me! But I get emails expressing as much.) If I can do this, there is certainly hope for you to do so too. I swear to you that anyone can learn to put on eye makeup (with practice), not eat horrible food all the time, keep a house reasonably tidy enough to enjoy spending time there, learn to dress in a way that is natural to you and be complimented on it, and be able to learn to socially interact with other humans and generally enjoy your life even when it's kind of a drag and a grind sometimes.

The trick is learning how to outsmart yourself and pinpointing what areas in your life need improvement. I learned that I liked running events because it made me feel in control. This made me less shy. Ditto for throwing parties. If I got too socially anxious at my own party, I could always hit the kitchen and people would understand. I like selling my goods in person because it's an easy way to talk to people. Outsmarting yourself won't be

48

perfect all the time. You'll backslide. You'll make mistakes. But, you'll figure it out. I have every faith and confidence in you.

Ritual Space

We've now been able to sort out your daily life reasonably well so that you are starting to feel in control of your immediate environment. Having this sorted means that we can move on to sorting your magical life. Does this mean that you can't do magic when you are a blubbering, desperate mess? No. Is it easier to do magic when you're reasonably in control of your situation? Yes. Think about it this way: People get jobs even when they are poorly dressed, desperate, and perhaps not even qualified or lacking in good social skills. But is it *significantly* easier when you are dressed nicely, can field interview questions, have the right qualifications, and remember to send a thank you note? Of course. That's the goal here: To make your life nicer and easier, as defined by you.

Where is your ritual space going to be? I find I do smaller workings by my altar at my dining room table which is where I consider my hearth to be centered. But, I do bigger, more secretive rituals in our spare room which Jow and I call Spare Oom from *The Lion, the Witch and the Wardrobe*, a favorite book for both of us (for Mr. Tummus and the wardrobe, less the Jesus-y bits). I find that when you can close a door and do magic in a confined space, it has a much more intense effect to the practitioner. Your space doesn't have to be big. It can be as small as your nightstand or your window ledge and it can also do double duty. We eat and entertain in our dining room as well as do our magical practice there. Whenever things get hectic, we tend to use Spare Oom as ad hoc storage space. Around Christmas, we have gifts to be given and to be received in there. Craft season finds Spare Oom littered with wool roving and various other beeswax flotsam and soap making jetsam. We try to keep it contained but we live in a small space and sometimes we just can't. But the key point to this is to try to do your rituals in one or two places in your home so that you start to build up an energetic resonance in that space. This makes doing magic easier. If you are lucky enough to have a space in your home solely dedicated to this purpose, even better.

If you've been practicing magic long enough, you likely have a good amount of out-of-commission magical tools and items. Like with the other aspects of your life, curating your items is a critical thing to do. If you don't, then you have the same pack rat problems you have in other areas of your life. Feel free to donate items that you have not used in any kind of recent memory and can bear to part with. Before donating, make sure to clean your items. If there are any spirits attached to your items, be sure to release them. If you have a few items that cannot be given to other people for whatever magical reasons you may have, be sure to place them at a cross roads or bury them, ideally with a mind towards being environmentally considerate. If they are just covered in your own personal magical energy/goop, consider placing these items in a bowl of sea salt before donating. Some people prefer to give items to other magical practitioners. Some people don't mind if they get donated with old clothes to Goodwill. I leave those personal decisions to you.

As a sidebar, if your ritual space is in your bedroom and other people reside there, it's a show of good manners to be considerate of the other people sleeping there--especially if they're magically inclined. There are spirits and gods that Jow works with that don't particularly agree with me on an energetic level. Does that mean he can't work with them? Of course not. Is it a nice thing to refrain from inviting these spirits and gods into our shared bedroom where I sleep at night? Yes. We have a rule: We have to agree on any kind of magical working and entity to be invited into that particular vulnerable shared space. If you sleep with a non-magically inclined person(s), they may not really care if the Elder Gods are cuddled up next to them in bed. But it's a nice thing to let anyone sharing a space with you know who *they're* sharing a space with.

One of the things I fell in love with through reading a mind-numbing amount of French aspirational books was the idea of shopping with purpose. I really liked the idea—especially in ritual practice. I'm not going to lie! When it comes to something like acquiring herbs, I have more of a Target/armful of sweaters approach to things. I tend to want herbs because I want them. I don't need to be sure of what I'm going to do with them. I'm sure I'll use them some day. For me, that's a reasonably true statement. Herbs come in pretty small packets that can be stored in one little bin. But when deciding about what should be a part of Spare Oom, both Jow and I decided we wanted to pull back from our typical American consumerist enthusiasm and be mindful about what lives in there.

While this may not serve a direct magical quid quo pro purpose per se, æsthetics are more important than you might think. Think about magical spaces (both fictional and real). Think about how you felt when you saw them or were in them. Did you feel that spark of energy? Did you feel like your mind opened up just a little more than it was before? Did you feel a surge of power? These are important aspects to both life and magic. Magic is supposed to help you be more awake and aware than the average person. Feeling inspired by art and beauty helps you get one step closer to that. Making art and beauty part of your magical practice not only feeds you energetically but also feeds you emotionally and spiritually. Doing something just because it creates beauty is something that we continue to devalue in business-oriented societies and even in a lot of magical theory. My thought? What has it ever hurt to really like the room you're in where you do magic?

Things to consider for your ritual space:

1. What kind of look are you going for in your ritual space? For us personally, we want it to feel like the Witches/Nurses Huts from *Sleep No More* only curated to fit in a modern condo and not freak out non-occults who visit our home. This is still a work in progress. Again, Pinterest is your friend and can help you move

around furniture online to figure out what you're looking for. For instance: Who would guess that we'd find the compartmentalized table we wanted at Pottery Barn?

2. Do you share this space? If so, it needs to be a neutral space energetically for all parties and/or may need to house other items from the rest of the household. Work with the others who share this space to figure out how to make it the best of both worlds so everyone's needs are met.

3. Does your ritual space have wood flooring for all sorts of super cool chalk markings? If not, consider using black Hawaiian salt to do any basic floor markings as it will show up against carpeting and is really easy to vacuum up. You could also get fabric to draw or embroider on for the floor.

4. Do you have a book case in your ritual space? If not, you may want to get one—even if it's a tiny Ikea one. It's nice to have your reference books close at hand. It also feels more occult-like. We have a large book case for Spare Oom. Half of it houses my craft business supplies (We live in a small space!) and the other half houses our most used reference books to make our lives easier.

5. Does your space have a surface for ritual-related items? We got a really cute little white faux French table from

Amazon. It works perfectly for the space and for our ritual work.

6. Do you have storage space for your ritual-related items? We store most of our stuff in the dining room altar. It is actually a baker's rack with two basket cubbies. We use the shelves for our deities and our non-ritual magical working space. We use the baskets to store our components. In Spare Oom, we keep a basket holding our ritual items. We have a small shelving unit that matches the table with more of our ritual components. We have small hooks hanging from it to hang dried herbs.

7. For general décor, consider what pictures you want hung in the room. We have a three-dimensional door knob/lock and key that we picked up at a thrift store, my Serial Killer/*The Secret*/Motivational Board, and a print from Sarah Lawless. I went on a terrarium spree so there's a bunch of those in there as well. In general, you can't go wrong having plants in a room meant for ritual space.

The Arte of Being a Host/ess

Now that we've gotten your living space sorted out, it may be a good time to talk about having people over in it. Knowing how to throw a killer party can help have an amazing ritual. Having a ritual and having a party require the same basic components. You need to have a nice space to have guests in, the guest list, there's food involved and etiquette to be aware of. If you can throw a nice party for people, you can have a nice ritual for spirits.

On the surface, throwing a party seems like a no-brainer sort of thing to do. But, there are a lot of nuances to it. The first aspect we will cover is the guest list. Is this a large party or a small party? I define a small party as less than ten people and a large party as more than ten people. When throwing an intimate dinner party, you want to choose your guest list very carefully so that you can make sure that there will be a lot of good conversation. If you select only shy introverts who don't really know each other, it's going to be a bit of an uphill battle to get some good conversation flowing. For a small party, you want to make sure to invite people who you think will have a good chemistry together and won't need a lot of "babysitting". You also want to make sure that they don't have any outstanding problems with each other that you know about. With a larger party that's not such a big deal because there are enough people for the feuding parties to avoid each other and circulate with other guests. It's assumed that the guests are adult enough to attend the party only if they feel they can handle being in the same room with the offending other party. You're looking to have a good time, not an episode of *The Real Housewives of Wherever*.

As the host/ess, it's your job to circulate among your guests and make sure that everyone has someone to talk to. If you see someone who doesn't know a lot of people, work her into a large group conversation. This can be done as simply as "Oh, tell Betty what you're talking about! I know she'd be interested." Or, with a little more skill, by listening to the conversation and considering what Betty could contribute to it, when there is a pause in the conversation, interject with something like, "Betty has this really great theory on why Ironman is more likable than Batman. Tell them about it, Betty!"

Ice breakers are really lame but there are a few things you can do if the party is not doing well. Sometimes, having a little activity like glittery temporary tattoos for people to paint on each other can make people socialize more because it's silly and ridiculous. Having a book like *If: Questions for the Game of Life* lying around for people to play with can be helpful too. If it's getting late and people just aren't socializing, a movie isn't the worst thing to try. If you hang out with a geeky crowd having a movie like *Twilight* with the RiffTrax (the guys from *Mystery Science Theater* started making them and they can be purchased for a couple dollars online.) set up can be fun.

The next thing to figure out is your menu. An occasional party where you keep things simple by having people bring a favorite wine and cheese (and you supply the paper goods, the fruit, the crackers, and a dessert) is fine—especially if you are your circle's primary party thrower. But, too much potluck tends to make people cranky. However, as my circle's primary party thrower, I can also tell you that having to shell out a massive amount of money every time you want to have cocktails with your friends gets cranky-making on the other side, too! So, the best bet is to split the difference, if you will. Having a simple menu such as an antipasto plate for appetizers, spaghetti with Marinara sauce with meatballs and turkey sausage for the dinner, a tiramisu cake for dessert and wine for drinks can keep the costs down. If your guests know what the menu is, they can add to whatever course they like or be content with what's being offered. Shopping at a grocery store that's more about volume sales than high-end produce can also keep costs down.

For a larger party, it's a good idea to assign a few of your nearest and dearest tasks to make sure everything runs smoothly. While you should always greet your guests personally, having a vivacious friend in charge of answering the door and introducing the guest around after you've greeted her is a huge help. Assigning someone to be in charge of bartending and minding the oven is really helpful. Bartending is good task for someone who's a little shy. It's a good way for her to mingle just by making drinks. This makes it easy for you to ensure that everything is going smoothly in terms of guests enjoying themselves and taking care of party administrative tasks such as making sure the food comes out when it's supposed to, that guests are having fun, room temperature and stereo volume are perfect.

Consider your home's ambiance for the party. There are a few things that you can do to make your life easy. Setting up a playlist for music is now really easy—thanks to services like Spotify. You want to start the music about a half hour before the guests are to arrive to get yourself in the party mood and because there's always an early bird. As there is always an early bird, make sure you're ready a half hour before the party starts so you don't make yourself crazy trying to entertain and finish getting ready. Figure out what you're wearing the day before to save yourself some sanity. When setting up your home, think about how to arrange chairs and tables so guests have enough room to circulate. Burning some nice incense an hour before the party is a good idea. Make sure your bathroom is stocked with paper goods and consider setting out an emergency basket so you don't have to hunt for anything for guests. My emergency basket always has: a new, unopened toothbrush, stockings in regular and queen size, small bottle of hairspray, a small first aid kit, allergy meds, aspirin, bobby pins, a lighter, a brush, a stain stick, antacid, anti-bacterial hand gel, tampons and pads. Vigil candles are inexpensive, found at your grocery store in the Latin Foods section, long burning and unlikely to set your house on fire so they're great to add a bit of mood lighting to your home. Ideally, your home should be cleaned and cleansed before the party as well.

Hosting a large ritual is similar to hosting a large party but with a few additional considerations thrown in. Generally, rituals in New Jersey are a pot luck affair which makes labeling each try of food with a post it with what it is and what's in it is a good idea. You don't need to go crazy. Just list common allergens. For example, pasta with meat sauce would be "Pasta with Meat Sauce: Gluten, beef, onion, garlic and wine, no nuts". It's also a good idea to assign someone who is both experienced with food prepping and the ritual format to the role of Kitchen Witch. In my grove, the Kitchen Witch labels all the food, figures out what food should be heated when, what food should be served when, and prepares the food for serving. Sometimes this is simple (cutting bread, slicing lasagna) and sometimes it's more complex (carving a goose). Our Kitchen Witch will also prepare plates for people with large ritual parts according to their wishes to help them ground and not have to worry about fighting their way to the kitchen table and being stopped every few feet to discuss the ritual. Unofficially, the Kitchen Witch also usually winds up with a lot of people in the cooking space pre-rit and post-rit to either hide a bit or to do some venting and possibly crying. It's a good idea for the Kitchen Witch to wear an apron for all of this. It's also a really good idea to make sure your Kitchen Witch is publicly thanked and appreciated at some point during the ritual or right before.

When leading a ritual, it's a very good idea to introduce new members to existing members so that they don't feel overwhelmed and/or left out. Assigning a Greeter is a good idea for a large ritual. It's also a really good idea to have a pre-ritual briefing talking about the holiday or reason you're having a ritual, a bit about your group, a bit about the deities that will be invoked, a bit about any kind of magical working you will be doing and discussing the ritual format. It's also typically a good idea with a large group to have a few Willow Priest/esses who can help people ground upon request and handle mundane issues like giving directions and answering the phone.

Being a Good Guest

Being a good guest is just as important as being a good host/ess, in my opinion. If you are going to a party where you don't know anyone but the host/ess, it's important not to monopolize her/his time. The host/ess will have a lot of things to see to. Sometimes, as the party winds down, she may have more time to spend with you. If you're planning on having a serious heart-to-heart with the host/ess, it's a good idea to arrange for a separate time to get together. If you are incredibly shy, it's a good idea to check the invitation to see if it's okay to bring someone with you so you have someone to talk to.

Even with bringing someone, be prepared to be friendly and engage in some of the conversations going on around you. If you are more introverted and all of that sounds like it would take too many spoons that particular week, you can always politely decline the invitation and suggest a time to get together with the host/ess.

Dressing appropriately is important, too. Generally, here, you have a lot more leeway than you would at a job interview or a funeral. If there's a theme, try to at least give a nod to it somehow in your attire. If you've never been to a party thrown by this particular host/ess, ask the hostess or a fellow party attendee what people generally wear to the party. You don't want to be completely over or under dressed.

If you ask your host/ess if she needs help and she declines, accept that gracefully. Try your best to arrive on time but not too early, unless requested by the host/ess. She may not be prepared to receive you early. Badgering your host/ess about how you can help just adds to her party-giving stress. Offer your help once and then leave it alone.

Never go to a party empty handed—even if you are told no gifts. Always bring a little gift for the host/ess. A bottle of wine, candles, a box of chocolates, flowers already in a vase, a hand-made item—things of that nature are always nice. The goal of the gift is so that the host/ess doesn't have to work too hard to display it or share it with her guests if she chooses to. Keep that in mind when choosing. Giving the host/ess a goose to cook and carve for the party isn't much of a gift in most cases due to how much work is required!

As for the age-old question of appropriate topics to engage in? That really varies from group to group. The best thing you can do is to observe what people are talking about and how they are discussing various topics and then dive in based on your observations. You may still make a faux pas, but most people are understanding—especially if there are cocktails involved. A party is not the place to get into a very heated debate, air social and personal grievances, or ask for professional advice from any of the party-goers.

Be sure to say good night and thank your host/ess when leaving for the evening. A thank you card, email, text, phone call, or even Facebook note is always a nice touch.

Being a good guest for a ritual isn't too different from being a good guest at a party. If your ritual is a potluck, and it is at all possible for you to do, a main dish is always especially appreciated. It could be a grocery store pre-made rotisserie chicken, some cold cuts and rolls or something you've personally made. Most people tend to bring chips or dessert which can be problematic when everyone wants to eat at the ritual feast. It's also problematic from a grounding perspective. A tray of mashed potatoes is far more useful for grounding purposes than a chocolate cake. It's not to say you can never bring a dessert. But, if you do, it's a nice idea to bring a main dish as well. Labeling your food ahead of time also makes less work for the kitchen witch. State the name of the food and list the ingredients. Those with food allergies will be most grateful.

Past that, show up on time (not to be confused with Pagan Standard Time) and bring an appropriate offering for the deity/ies being honored. Offer to help, but politely accept it if help is not needed. Do some research on the group you're attending, the holiday you're celebrating (if applicable), and the deities you're honoring. This helps the ritual go better for all participants. If there are ritual parts you can volunteer for on the day of the ritual and you feel comfortable doing so, it's a nice thing to do so that the Priest/ess isn't floundering to find enough people to make the ritual go.

If you have grievances with other parties attending the

ritual, ritual space is not the best place in most circumstances to air them. If the idea of being in a closed circle with Nancy makes you want to claw your own eyes out and you know Nancy is attending, don't attend.

I think the subject of an open ritual space/closed ritual space (i.e. a ritual format where you can't leave during the ritual versus a ritual format where you can come and go as you please during the ritual) is important to consider when you have grievances with other members of your group. If it's an open space, I personally find it doesn't feel so claustrophobic to share it with people you have issues with. If it does feel claustrophobic, you can step outside at any time to get some air. If it's a more minor grievance with someone you have issues with, you may be okay to share a closed ritual space with that person and then do what my grove calls "rit 'n run", meaning you stay for the ritual itself and then head out.

Sometimes the social part of the ritual feasting can be more stressful than the ritual itself if you have issues with some of the members. In my experience, at least, don't attend a ritual that is led by someone you have ongoing issues with. It's not nice for you. It's not nice to the energy of the group, and it's not nice to the host. You probably care the least about the person you have the issues with in that situation but if you have the good manners not to attend, then, that other person will likely have the good manners not to attend when you are running a ritual. So, it's a quid quo pro situation.

If you find yourself particularly ungrounded in a ritual and there's no willow priest/ess and you don't know anyone there, it's okay to ask the leader of the group for help in getting back on the ground. If you would prefer to ground yourself out, things that often help are eating some salt, checking the time, talking about mundane things, changing clothes, or eating starchy food. Generally, things will dissipate reasonably within a few hours. Don't drive if you're ungrounded. It's a terrible idea.

Before or after ritual, it's okay to ask questions about the ritual if you're unclear on a point. But, don't interrupt the ritual and don't derail a pre-ritual briefing. If you're worried about being uncomfortable during the ritual and that you may want to leave, privately ask the ritual leader beforehand what the protocol is for that situation.

All of the Things

Getting all these aspects of your daily life in order is not something that can be accomplished overnight of course. It's going to be a work in progress to get everything the way you want it to be. You're going to slip up and not be as on top of everything as you want to be. You're going to eat things you're not proud of, you're going to skip yoga one night, it's all part of the process. The goal is to enjoy living your life more, not to become a Stepford Wife Occult Automation. One night you may enjoy reading Mormon Mommy Blogs more than doing laundry. *Pourquoi pas?* As the French would say! The goal is to find that delicate balance between Accomplishing All the Things All the Time and

Accomplishing None of the Things None of the Time. You're smart and capable, you can do this.

CHAPTER IV

The Arte of the Ladies

A Primer on Working with the Ladies

Some schools of magical thought suggest you use a circle to work with spirits so you can entrap them and bend them to your will. This is an excellent approach if most of the spirits you work with are dangerous gun-toting drug dealers who you owe $10,000. In my daily life, I tend to invite into my house people who have a decent enough reputation in my circles and/or I have reason to trust. I would prefer to offer guests in my home a glass of wine and a nice nibble rather than tying them to a chair and beating them over the head repeatedly. I feel it's more hospitable.

I don't tend to run with people I can't trust in my daily life. I don't really feel the need to go down other-worldly dark alleys for the things I need. Does this mean you should have perfect love and perfect trust for the spirits you work with? I take a middle ground there, too. In my daily life, I tend to have what I consider moderate trust for people, based on my relationship with them.

Is the thought always in the back of my mind that each

person in my life could turn on me, cut me out of their lives, steal from me, or otherwise act terribly to me for some reason, at some point? Yes. Do I let that thought be any more than something to keep in the back of my head until I have reason to think otherwise? No. I'm cautiously optimistic with other people. I like to think that people I have a relationship with love me and want what's best for me. But, I'm not so naive or trusting that I think that others don't have their own thoughts, feelings, and agendas.

I treat my relationships with my spirits the same way. My work with spirits, gods, and otherworldly entities is reflective of this ideal. I use a method of creating a circular sacred space, but it's so that my spirits can more easily manifest themselves. Its purpose is not to entrap them and force my will upon them.

Like everything else in this book, engage your brain and your common sense. Are the Ladies dangerous? Yes and no. A person, generally speaking, isn't dangerous unless you give her a reason to be. If you take someone out of her home, throw a black bag over her head, toss her into a van, and threaten her, she's probably going to be dangerous. If a friend has introduced you to someone and you into your home, make her a cup of tea, and treat her politely, it's unlikely that she will be dangerous. You've shown her you have manners and hospitality. Is that a blood oath that the person your friend introduced to you and that you allowed in your home won't steal your silver and your cat? Of course not! It's *possible* this person will do something terrible, but it's not terribly likely.

Consider me the friend who is introducing you to the Ladies. I'm telling you the things that They tend to like and urging you to be polite and mannerly. If you don't treat them politely, then whatever happens happens. If you are polite, you most likely won't have any problems.

Can I absolutely positively promise you will have no problems, that you'll hit it off, and that you'll get everything you ever wanted ever? No. Of course not! The Ladies are spirits, not gumball machines. No one can make that promise with any flesh-and-blood person. Why would that be the case with a spirit?

Welcome to the real world! The magical world isn't that much different. But I *can* help you put your best foot forward. You may have a better or easier relationship with some of the Ladies over the others, just like people in your daily life. That's okay too.

With the Ladies, you don't want to start your relationships by making a huge show of power and telling them you're in charge of them. First off, would you like that in your daily life? How would you feel if I showed up to your cubicle randomly and informed you that I'm your new boss and I can kick your ass any time I want? As your new boss, would I demand you immediately give me everything I request or I'm going to kill one of your family members? You'd think I was a lunatic! Unless you're working with spirits who are the equivalent to dangerous drug dealers, they're going to think the same thing.

Moreover, why would you take that approach with any

flesh-and-blood person who is more powerful than you? It doesn't seem like the smartest way to handle things. You would want to charm that flesh-and-blood person and make them want to be your friend and want to do things for you. If you took that aggressive approach with a flesh-and-blood person from whom you needed a favor, she would probably crush you just out of sheer principle for being such a ridiculous asshole to her. Guess what? If you need help from a god or a spiritual entity, She's more powerful than you. Trufax, as they say on the intertubes. It's why you're asking Her for help in the first place.

I prefer to have spiritual relationships based on a reasonable amount of love and trust. First off, it's hard to work with anyone (flesh and blood or spirit) when you can't get along or you can't trust each other. So, it's better to work with spirits with whom you can build a relationship by increasing respect, trust, and affection. Secondly, let's say you need a hundred dollars. Who do you think is going to be more likely to lend it to you, give it to you, or help you get it in some way: A stranger off the street or a close friend or family member? Exactly! Make friends. Know your own boundaries. Be nice.

I shy away from the word "archetype" when describing the Ladies. It makes them sound like they're not actual individual spirits. They are. But I feel each Lady is closer to The Morrigan or Cernunnos in Celtic mythos where The Morrigan/Cernunnos isn't so much the name for those specific deities so much as it is a job title. Going with that, my Morrigan in my local Morrigan "office" may be somewhat different from your Morrigan in your Morrigan's local "office". They both will do the same job (wash the clothes of the dead, be present for our battles) but my Morrigan may have red hair, enjoy whiskey, and love industrial music. Your Morrigan may be blond, listen to Mozart, and prefer port wine. Both do the same job, both are real spirits. It's sort of like how Becky in Accounting in the New Brunswick office does the same job as Susan does in Accounting in the Trenton office. They are two completely different people doing the same job. Your Ladies may have somewhat different likes and dislikes from my Ladies. Although the appearance of your Ladies may be differ from my Ladies, all Ladies in Red will fulfill the same general spiritual job function regardless to specific details. As such, I'm painting each Lady in broad enough strokes so that you can find your own individual Ladies with whom to work. I filled in enough detail that you will recognize each Lady you encounter in your work by their spiritual job functions, general appearances, and general preferences.

Magic Herself

Gates are a concept in many magical traditions. For me, notably, it's the ADF Druidry ritual format. Whenever and however you first learn to open the gates between the worlds—be it casting a circle or doing a gate opening—the first few times felt like this to me: *This is serious magical business. I, Deborah Castellano, have done magic. I created this space between worlds.*

70

I am amazing.

Eventually, you learn that gates and doors between the worlds are happening all the time. They're constantly opening and closing naturally or through magical means. You do want a door to open between the worlds in your rite. It will be how the Ladies will enter into your ritual. Opening the door between the worlds will also make your magic more powerful because it will be happening in between this world and the other world. You'll be setting up a liminal space. This is the best kind of space for spirit work and magic.

You could, of course, open the space yourself. But it's a lot harder that way because you don't have anyone to help you open the door from the other side of it. It would be helpful and wise to use a gatekeeper. I recommend asking the spirit I call Magic Herself for help.

What She's Like

You'll try to leave a trail of breadcrumbs to find her, but Magic Herself is trickier than that. She's seen all your stupid mortal tricks before. Sometimes, her hair is long and raven with twigs and sprigs of rosemary in it. Sometimes, she wears a long, blue velvet dress. Sometimes, she waits for you at the bottom of the lake, her blond hair braided with kelp, a sword clutched in her hand. Sometimes, she has blue eyes, burning with fire. Sometimes, her eyes are as dark as the forest, deep as the ocean. Sometimes, she is as pale as wheat. Sometimes, she has cafe mocha dreadlocks, her skin as dark as the bear's fur that she wears.

71

Sometimes, she wears scraps of leather that she's sewn together out with your sinew. Sometimes, she lives in a house that smells like ginger and nutmeg, past where the bare trees scratch against each other, shivering in the cold. Her house is the color of firelight. Her laugh is like a fox's bark. She'll invite you in. Her oven gleams warm and bright. She knows your secret desires. She knows what makes you desperate. She knows what makes you burn.

What She Does

Magic Herself opens gates. Magic Herself closes doors. Magic Herself guards your back in the ways between the worlds. Magic Herself shows you the underpinnings of your magic. She teaches you how to make your magic stronger. Magic Herself guides your hand during a ritual. She makes introductions. She carries your magic to the appropriate parties.

What She Likes

Magic Herself likes white candles, teacups, milk and honey. She craves clean water offerings. She likes waterhouse pictures, dragon's blood, knives, daggers and cloaks. Magic Herself desires white sapphire.

Her Invocation
Magic Herself

Lady of doorways, Lady of lakes
Orphic Lady
Lady of darkness and light

Spirit of sorcery
Lady of hidden paths
She Who Enchants
She Who Opens the Way
She Who Instructs
Come, Fair Lady,
Come, Lady of Openings and Closings
Favor me with your presence

Her Glyph

The Lady in Red
What She's Like

The Lady in Red is in the back of the club where you have to know someone who knows someone who knows someone who knows someone to be allowed to drink handcrafted small batch gin martinis. No suits allowed. The price of admission is only a memory or a dream. The Lady in Red is a multi-platinum pop singer, dressed in black swan feathers, cleverly singing about social issues in rhyme. She has the ear of the king as she is his favorite mistress. The Lady in Red is swathed in Dior. She wears emeralds the size of goose eggs on fingers that are always typing on her iPhone. When she was young, The Lady in Red went to bed with her stomach hollow with hunger every night. Everyone else may have forgotten her poverty, but she never has. Bare-backed, in a long, satin, blood-red gown dripping in diamonds, her strawberry curls in disarray, she eats raw meat with her hands. She runs the show and everybody knows it from the cops to the dons. The Lady in Red makes the rules. She decides when to break them. Everything is permitted until she says otherwise. Her table is in the back; her back is against the wall. With the flick of her finger, The Lady in Red will allow you to join her. She'll know exactly who you are before you even open your mouth. Everything has a price and she knows yours. Do you?

What She Does

The Lady in Red loves, lusts. She puts people together. She tears people apart. The Lady in Red is a master of the art of the charm. She has perfected the art of the con. The Lady in Red knows how to be perfectly *charming.* She knows about the glamour of your physical appearance. The Lady in Red is the mistress of the party. She is the patron of the host/ess. The Lady in Red is the spirit of sensuality, poetry, song. She is the mistress of love making, of fucking. and fucking someone over.

What She Likes

The Lady in Red likes garnets, rubies, champagne and dark chocolate. The Lady in Red desires fur, velvet, oysters and white gardenias. She loves the opera, live music, red candles, gowns, dancing, perfume, red meat and French pastries.

Her Invocation

Lady of the back rooms, Lady of the speak easy

Scarlet Lady

Lady of trickery and deceit

Spirit of flaming desire

Lady of hollow'd hunger

She Who Burns

She Who Inspires

She Who Charms

Come, Glorious Lady,

Come, Lady of the Ways

Favor me with your presence

Her Glyph

The Lady of the Hearth

What She's Like

The Lady of the Hearth is the glowing, pregnant woman who is effortless in your yoga class. Her parties always go until three in the morning. The Lady of the Hearth always has enough blankets and pillows for everyone. She pays her rent by brewing her own beer and curing her own meat in her apartment in Brooklyn. The Lady of the Hearth's chestnut brown hair shines and her face is lovely and lineless. Her little girls dress in high heels and the MAC lipstick she no longer has the patience to wear. They eat cookies in her bed, snuggling next to her telling her, "Mommy, I love you." The Lady of the Hearth's black plastic glasses always look chic. She carefully balances her budget, puts money into her Roth IRA, and makes her famous Creole jambalaya. There is always enough jambalaya for everyone.

The Lady of the Hearth invites you into her home. It is decorated just the way you always wanted yours to be. She serves all of your favorite food. Her outfit is the perfect weekend casual.

She has a successful career in her passion. You must ask The Lady of the Hearth for help if you want it. If you can swallow your pride and find the courage, she'll freely share with you everything you need to know. Will you ask?

What She Does

The Lady of the Hearth does large and small prosperity magic. She is adept at the art of likeability. She can smooth out family relations. The Lady of the Hearth will enchant your food. She is the mistress of the arts of cooking, housekeeping, and brewing. The Lady of the Hearth is the glamour of having everything you need already. She is the epitome of calmness and competence. The Lady of the Hearth is the mistress of your finances. She is the art of making a house a home.

What She Likes

The Lady of the Hearth likes fresh-baked bread and muffins, stout beer, kitchens, and aprons. Yet she also likes spreadsheets, local and sustainable items, and beeswax candles. She adores handspun yarn, fresh herbs, and food you've made by your own hand. She likes wildflowers, and apples. The Lady of the Hearth demands cleanliness and organization. She prefers Martha Stewart/Real Simple magazines, shabby chic, brown topaz, and brown candles.

Her Invocation

Lady of domesticity, Lady of the home
Vibrant Lady
Lady of plenty and contentment

Spirit of the home fire

Lady of the harvest

She Who Listens

She Who Gifts

She Who Gives Birth

Come, Glowing Lady

Come, Lady of Cups

Favor me with your presence

Her Glyph

The Lady of the Wood
What She's Like

The leather boots of The Lady of the Wood are silent as she cocks an arrow in her bow, sending it flying into the heart of the white stag. She carefully drinks from his heart's blood as she breaks down the stag into parts for eating and for household goods. Nothing will be wasted. Her midnight hair is neatly braided.

The Lady of the Wood looks timeless in her Calvin Klein suit as she finishes her Power Point presentation to her new employees at the company she has just obtained. Everyone's new responsibilities are neatly outlined along with the corporate culture and personal benefit improvements that they could expect.

Your footfalls are too loud. You smell too freshly of soap and human. You've never used a bow before. You'll starve to death if you don't learn how to kill with speed, compassion, and focus. The Lady of the Wood will teach you everything you need to survive in the boardroom and the woods. But, her lessons don't come without sacrifice. What are you willing to lay down to become the hunter?

What She Does

The Lady of the Wood is art of the kill. She is the glamour of the hunt. The Lady of the Wood is the epitome of art of survival. She is the personification of agility, focus, and cunning. The Lady of the Wood can teach you how to protect yourself and others. She is strategy and stillness. The Lady of the Wood can teach you how to become the hunter not the hunted. The Lady of the Wood is fearlessness. She is the depths of your own power and strength. The Lady of the Wood is endurance. She stands for what it means to be brave.

What She Likes

The Lady of the Wood likes bows, arrows, and leather. She enjoys spiced wine, dried meat, good cheese, and clean water. She loves to dress in warm clothes and warm boots. She craves green peridot and thick hand lotion. The Lady of the Wood loves to drink mead. Some of her favourite things include: throwing knives, green candles, puzzles, Sudoku, hounds, beeswax lip balm, and herbal tinctures.

Her Invocation

Lady of the Hunt, Lady of the Kill

Cunning Lady

Lady of silence and speed

Lady of the knave

She Who Survives

She Who Preserves

She Who Protects
Come, Graceful Lady
Come, Lady of the Beast
Favor me with your presence

Her Gylph

The Lady of the Mysteries
What She's Like

No one has ever seen the inside of stately old Victorian house at the end of the block. It is owned by a graceful, silver-haired woman. Her house is not in perfect condition but not in disrepair either.

Vaguely, some remember that she used to be a nose for Chanel. Or was she a designer for Hermes? Wasn't she a nurse during a war? Didn't she dance with a ballet company? Late at night, the desperate, the daring and the dumb will knock on her back door looking for her help. They wait outside in the smothering humidity, or the numbing cold until she has prepared what they are looking for. A tiny glittering vial. A hollow egg. A packet of pungent herbs. She asks the questions. It is not for others to question her.

The Lady of the Mysteries is the silent matriarch, swathed in black. She speaks only the language of the country she left, constantly stirring her pot with the spoon. Her tiny figure refuses to be bent. It commands respect and a stirring of fear across the back of the necks of all who cross her path. The Lady of the Mysteries is unbending. Her heart is full of the secrets of the dead generations that came before her. She will never share these secrets until the proper time.

What She Does

The Lady of the Mysteries is the art of forgiveness. She is the glamour of experience, the art of the hex and the jinx. The Lady of the Mysteries is mistress of the hidden and unseen. She is the personification of death and dying arts. The Lady of the Mysteries is the mistress of letting go, of holding on, of tenaciousness, and change. She is the keeper of the forgotten. She personifies hard-won wisdom, traditions old and new, and silence. She is the heart of the darkness, prophecy and scrying.

What She Likes

The Lady of the Mysteries likes ink, paper, dried flowers and herbs. She enjoys tobacco, black candles, black pearls, port wine and whiskey. She has an appreciation for antique teacups, henbane, blood, vintage brooches and tea. One of her favourite foods is duck or goose. The Lady of the Mysteries likes black scrying vessels, pins, needles, thimbles, and gloves with buttons. Invite her for tea sandwiches and sweets.

Her Invocation

Lady of enigmas, lady of the unknown
Clandestine lady

Lady of the unseen and hidden

Lady of Experience

She Who Curses

She Who Forgives

She Who Remembers

Come, Elegant Lady

Come, Lady of Darkness

Favor me with your presence

Her Glyph

Daring, Cunning and Brave

Each Lady will teach you something different and will bring something unique to your magical practice and daily life. Like a flesh-and-blood person, they are complicated and come to you are fully developed beings with their own agendas. Strive to build a relationship with each of them in the ritual format outlined in the following chapter and see what doors open up to you. Your cake is baked, it's time for the fondant.

CHAPTER V

The Arte of Ritual

A Whole Day's Work

When I do the ritual format I'm sharing with you in this book, I give myself a full day for everything from setting up Spare Oom to gathering items to my beauty regimen to the ritual itself to ritual decompression. I enter the space feeling calm and centered. I leave the space knowing I gave my ritual my full attention for the day and created something beautiful just for myself and my spirits. It's like an amazing secret society that I'm the only (human) member of.

When I do this rite, I give myself permission to create beauty for myself and my spirits. Since it's temporary (I dismantle the altar the next day.) and private, it's sort of like my own personal mini Burning Man in that it's about creating beauty for the sake of beauty and not for the sake of others. Creating beauty is so critical for our souls. Sadly, it's also the first thing we're willing to throw away for some reason. It's really easy to get worn down by day-to-day drudgery. Between endless piles of laundry, dishes, and the work commute, we can become disconnected from our spiritual selves all too quickly. Maybe you can't take a full day because you have children or a startup business. But, you need to block out as much time for this as you can possibly allow.

By giving yourself and your spirits this block of time, you're making a sacrifice to your spirits before the ritual even starts. It's hard to be undistracted. There's always Facebook bantering, someone's mini-emergency, texting, television, reading blogs, and becoming generally inattentive to what's really important. This is far from a new problem. Ennui has existed in various forms ever since society began. Even the gods in a lot of pantheons get distracted at times. (The Greek gods are infamous for this.)

Again, does that mean that magic can't happen without a full day of prep? No. My Dianic circles are always held on Fridays. It's pretty impossible not to skitter into the ritual with the potluck clasped in my teeth and ritual supplies shoved in my purse, feeling harassed and hassled from my day at work and dealing with traffic. I'm burnt out and stressed out. It's not the best way to go into a ritual. Do we make it work? Of course! But, what I'm proposing to you for the purpose of the ritual format in this book is to give yourself as much time as possible to lose yourself in the beauty of planning and executing a ritual.

What Are You Wearing?

We've discussed previously how what you're wearing affects your daily life. Now it's time to take that to the next level and discuss apparel for your ritual. Ideally, this ritual is about expressing yourself with a suggested structure to achieve your goals on a spiritual and magical level. What you wear to do magic is important. Magic is what you do to manipulate your surroundings in great and subtle ways. Shouldn't doing an act that powerful demand that you give at least as much thought to what you wear in ritual space as you do to a job interview? I thought about a ritual robe. It works for a lot of people—especially in high magic tradition. There's a level of internal "this is serious shit" associated with Gandolf and Merlin and other media depicted magic users. Ritual robes conjure up ideas of hoods and secrecy. Cloaks and daggers!

And bathrobes.

I really looked into getting a ritual robe. There are lots of people who design beautiful ones that look as masculine or feminine or anything in between as you like. But, I couldn't get past feeling like: "Is this what you do? Play dress up in your closed little room? How very..." Robes felt like drag in a bad way to me. I tried a nude ritual because the Lady I was working with felt it was important for me to be vulnerable and primal like that. I did it. At first, it was awesome! Look at me, acting like Ye Olde Witch! Being nude and sexy doing hot witchy things! Yeah! And then it felt sort of sweaty and uncomfortable. I didn't have any pockets. I couldn't really wipe my hands on anything. I was worried about dropping a hot charcoal on myself, which got distracting. I wasn't distracted by being self-conscious of my body so much as what my body was doing and how sticky it felt without clothes. None of this is intended to discourage you at all from buying yourself a lovely robe or going au naturale—if that's what you feel in your heart. Quite the contrary! I just want to share my personal journey to my ritual clothes to show you that it wasn't effortless and seamless. It's okay to try a few things out and see what works and what doesn't. You're captain of your own ship, after all. Finally, I personally decided on a few things concerning what I needed in ritual clothes:

1. I needed my ritual clothes to be black. I wanted to be able to wipe my hands on my clothes during ritual and for that not be a big deal.

2. I needed my ritual attire to be something that I could reserve just for rituals. I didn't want my ritual clothes to be covered in cat hair and daily life residue. Whenever I put it on, I wanted to associate it with ritual. I wanted it to retain the energy of the rituals I have done in the past so that it would accumulate magical energy.

3. I needed what I wore for the ritual to be aesthetically pleasing to my style sensibility. If aesthetics are to be an important part of daily and ritual practice, then my ritual clothes should reflect that. The best way to describe my personal style sensibility is taking an orphan from a rich family from the Victorian Era and shaking her in a box with Joan Holloway from *Mad Men*. I can't dress like this every day because of baby fluids. But, for ritual wear, I

really want to embrace my aesthetic. Naturally, my first thought was: Oh, too bad! I don't have anything at all like this! I guess I'll have to go shopping! But I'm planning a wedding this year and am still a fairly new homeowner. Once I started looking into what my Muse thought I should be wearing and more to the point, how much that dog and pony show was going to cost, it was time to go shopping in my own closet. I had a dress that I liked and couldn't quite part with but couldn't find the right occasion to wear it. It was a bit ubergoth for coffee at Starbucks. But, at the same time, it was a little low key for my now rare pilgrimages to places where I can get completely decked out. It's a simple, knee length, black chiffon dress with spaghetti straps with bib ruffles and jet buttons. I found an inexpensive black lace shrug that I wear with it so I'm not distracted by issues with my arms. Everything is machine washable. I generally wear my Gingersnaps style resin crow skull necklace with it and my fanciest French underthings. I keep my feet bare so I can feel connected to the earth better through my carpet. (Whatever! It works.) My ritual outfit makes me feel sexy, competent, and ready to do business with the spirit world.

Ritual Items and Space

As we've discussed before, you don't need a full room dedicated to magic at all times. But I do find a house does have a sort of ebb and flow for where magic happens. Our dining room is where our altar lives. So, we make our offerings to our gods there. It's where smaller magics—such as pooja work and hoodoo work—tend to be performed. Nothing really happens in the kitchen itself (which is different from our last place where the kitchen was where a lot of magic happened). Nothing happens in the living room (which isn't surprising because we're complete sloths there! We do work to keep the energy flowing despite our naughty laziness there). The bathroom is for cleansings/beauty regimen and the bedroom is for any sex based magic and some beauty regimen work. Any magic done in the bedroom must be cleared with the other party before it happens. That leaves Spare Oom for my ritual work. I really like doing the ritual I've created there for a few reasons. It's small enough to really get energy moving easily, all my magical items are in there. I can shut my blinds and get incense really going in there and I can shut the door.

Spare Oom seals really well and I find creating a seal for this particular ritual layout really does make a difference in the work. I never notice how big a difference it makes until I step out of Spare Oom and I stumble out to the house. There's a definite change in energy. After my ritual work, I make sure there's nothing left burning in there and then seal it off from the house overnight before taking apart the altar. I find the Ladies like having the evening to themselves in there to socialize. It makes the work more potent. If you can make that happen, I really recommend doing so. I had decided to shop thoughtfully for my ritual items because I wanted my ritual items to be another extension of my aesthetic. A mood board on Pinterest can really help you figure out what you are trying to accomplish.   My ritual aesthetic is *Sleep No More* meets country French Chic. It took me a while to figure out what that actually meant. I thought it would be more second hand shops and antiquing. However, it turns out that's really time consuming and not as inexpensive as you would think. So, really, while I got some of my items that way, most of my items were acquired through Anthropologie, Amazon, Etsy, and Pottery Barn. It's not as sexy or indie to say that. But, I got the things that I really wanted that way. Regardless of whether you shop in your own closet, in a tiny boutique in Paris, or at Target, I recommend taking your time with acquiring your ritual items so you can make sure that your aesthetic is being properly expressed.

For this ritual format you will need:

- Four vessels with lids: one filled with rain water, one filled with dirt close to your house, one with at least one feather found near your home and one with a candle (homemade by you if possible).
- A candle for your Lady of choice.
- A representation of your Lady of choice (picture, etc.)
- A candle for Magic Herself.
- A representation of Magic Herself.
- Offerings for your Lady of choice.
- Offerings for Magic Herself.
- A small table—round is best.
- At least one tablecloth—possibly to be decorated or

embroidered as you feel called to do so.

- A small salt cellar.
- Salt (I recommend Black Hawaiian).
- Incense (I recommend The Witch of Forest Grove's blends).
- Sage smudge.
- A cordial-sized glass for the Ladies.
- A cup for yourself.
- A small offering bowl or plate.
- A ritual dagger or wand that will be an extension of your will.
- A bowl for your incense.
- Charcoal.
- Fire source.
- Divination tool of your choice.

For my personal ritual items, I have a small, white, round, French style table from Amazon, four different colored jars numbered 1 through 4 that say "Plein de Bonnes Choses" (Plenty of Good Things) with lids from Anthropologie, a small glass bowl and cordial glass that I found at a second hand store, a tiny glass and gold antique salt cellar I got from Etsy, a black glass goblet I got from Target, a selection of incenses from The Witch of Forest Grove. My tablecloths come from my fabric bin and I use my curved sickle that I got from a witch store in New Hope when I was a baby Pagan and then promptly barely used.

Mind-Altering Substances

Substances like booze, pot, peyote, 'shrooms, X, salves, and marijuana have all been used in ritual space for however long it took for humans to realize it could be used to get high and/or alter your brain. Generally, in a mainstream, magic-based book, this is where you get a boring lecture on how drugs are bad. Mmmkay? And if you're a real occultist, you wouldn't need them! You likely double-plus don't need whatever pharmacopeia of drugs you're prescribed through your doctor/The Man. All you need is a positive attitude and a drum!

Bullshit.

First off, do you really think our ancestors were busy being the morality police on each other about whatever they were tripping out on during ritual space? No. If you didn't drop dead during or immediately after, it was a win.

OMG! Deb says it's okay to do drugs! I'm going to go out and do a bunch! No. Deb is not saying it's okay to do drugs. I am saying like with magic, you need to inject some common sense here. I am also not saying you have to do any kind of substance to do magic. 75% of my group ritual experience has been stone-cold sober. There's nothing wrong with that. But, in being so militant that no one is to use substances ever including perfectly legal substances, I feel a lot of practitioners are never taught how to use common sense with them.

Common Sense Rules for Mind-Altering Substances

1. It is not wrong to take medication that is prescribed to you by a

legitimate doctor who understands your medical history and the way your body reacts to medication. There's this horrible meme that's really prevalent especially in the occult community that if you take medication for anything, but especially for depression or anxiety, you are a Bad, New-Age Pony and aren't trying hard enough and should be able to magically rewire your brain chemistry so that you never need anything starting with an "X" or "P" because people who take Prozac or Xanax are completely numb from their problems! Kittens, I take both. If that were true, I'd sleep a lot better at night. My meds which I take for depression, anxiety, and fibromyalgia make it so I'm a functional human being who can do productive things in society. I can feel feelings, write, charm, hex, and hold down a day job. Anyone who tells you taking meds will make you comfortably numb so nothing bothers you and you won't be able to do anything productive is lying or on the wrong meds/dosage. Do I think everyone should be medicated? Of course not! But we do live in a first world country. If you can't function well, meds should be an option and one you shouldn't have to feel guilty or bad about. I think everyone should be able to do what they want with their bodies. Take meds. Don't take meds. Whatever! As long as you get to be the captain of your own ship and do what's best for you and your body. Not sure about one doctor's diagnosis or medicine-based regimen? Get a second or third opinion until you feel confident about what you're doing. See some alternative medical practitioners. You don't have to choose to be only Western-medicine based or alternative-medicine based if you don't want to.

2. If you are taking a regimen of prescribed medications or even vitamin and herbal supplements, you need to know what kind of substances you can take in combination. Some have very serious and potentially deadly interactions with each other. Acting out Uma Thurman's infamous scene from *Pulp Fiction* won't bring you closer to a magical awakening. It will just send you to the hospital.

3. Certain substances are illegal in some countries or states. Most have age restrictions attached to them. Check your local law before deciding what you want to use as part of your practice. If your substance of choice is illegally obtained, you could wind up with hefty fines, a criminal record, or jail time. There are many substances that are perfectly legal to use and will do the same thing.

4. Make sure you get your substances from a reputable source. You want to make sure your substance does what it's supposed to do.

5. Mind-altering substances are like dim sum. If you order twenty-two steamed buns and can't finish them, you can't undo ordering them. You have to pay for them. If you order four and want another two later, you can always order more. In other words, you can always start with one shot of vodka, see how you feel, give it some time to interact with your body, and then see if you want another shot. If you start with six, that party is in progress and you can't really undo it.

The goal in using any kind of mind-altering drug in ritual practice is simple: It's to put you in an altered state. It's not to get you high, drunk, or sloppy. It's to lower barriers that you may have to make your work more powerful for you. It's not so that you have no barriers or common sense. You still need to be in control of both your ritual and your senses. It can be a tricky process figuring out that spot between becoming more receptive to the ritual process and being unable to even get the ritual started. You need to know your body. Again, it's always better to start with less than with more.

7. Can't use mind-altering substances? Don't want to? Guess what? You don't have to!

It's just one way to get into a ritual head space. Lots of other things will accomplish that too like drumming, chanting and singing. There is nothing wrong with preferring to be sober. You're in charge of your body. If you would like to use a salve, I can personally recommend The Witch of Forest Grove's salves for this ritual format. None of the salves I've used have interacted badly with my medications (the same may not be true for yours, check with a professional first) and work really nicely for my work with the Ladies. I recommend Aves Flying Ointment for The Lady in Red, Fairy Ointment for Lady of the Wood, Toadman's Salve for Lady of the Hearth and Henbane Ointment for Lady of the Mysteries.

Beauty Regimen

In my year of reading French aspirational books, one of the

things that fascinated me the most is the idea of spending time tending to your own inner garden. This is a pastime that is supposedly highly touted among the French. As an American, it can be hard to translate. I'm about as solitary as a herd animal, generally speaking, and I have a lot of important reality television to watch. I'm a little sketchy as to what one's inner garden entails. But, it seems to be about spending time alone doing the things you want to do. And as a French woman (supposedly), one of the things you want to spend a lot of time doing is beautifying yourself.

I've grilled Euro friends on this extensively and it seems to be true enough, as much as any generality is. The French are famous for their drugstores. These aren't like an American drugstore but apparently full of potions and elixirs to make you beautiful and healthy with salesladies to tell you how to do better at being pretty, basically, and to scold you if you're not taking care of yourself properly. I'm scared of hair stylists and manicurists! I don't think I'd have the nerve to deal with French drugstore personnel. But I do think self-care is something that gets neglected a lot in America. Spending time beautifying yourself besides basic makeup application and hair styling is often sneered at and disparaged as something that spoiled rich ladies do.

While rich ladies have always had more access to bathing in general, bathing and ritual work has gone together in just about every world religion. It's certainly not something limited to people who identify as female. The Jewish faith has mikvahs. Mary

Magdalene washed Jesus' feet with her hair. Modern Wicca often incorporates bathing into pre-ritual preparation. I have found that incorporating pre-ritual cleansing into the formal rite I have made makes a drastic difference in how I go into my rite. There's a meditative aspect to spending time cleansing—not to mention the spiritual benefit of cleansing yourself both physically and spiritually before a ritual. It gives you a clean slate to work with for your ritual so that you're not dragged down with pre-existing negative energy that we all accumulate from the stress and strain of every-day life. Beauty regimen (as I call it) also gives you a chance to start easing into ritual space before the ritual even starts. I don't know about you, but if I have time to shave my legs in the shower it's a massive win for me during the week. I don't often have very much time to dedicate to beautifying/cleansing. I, personally, chose to stubbornly call this aspect of pre-ritual prep Beauty Regimen in the blogosphere. I don't see what's wrong with making yourself feel beautiful using semi-traditional means for religious purposes.

Again, it's nothing new. Wearing your Sunday Best for church is a long-held custom in America. Ditto for most other world religions. If I could spend an hour getting ready for a date, why shouldn't I give my spirits the same courtesy to put my best foot forward? Also, I find it just feels different doing magic with no makeup, my hair pulled back in a ponytail, and sweats versus when I take the time and energy to spruce myself up pre-ritual. For me, it shows intent before I've even begun. I've given up this block of time that could be spent surfing on the Intertubes and being mentally checked out on my time off to instead plug in and dedicate time and energy to my personal spiritual practice for no other reason than because it creates beauty for me. It gives me new perspective on my life, and it gives me a sense of peace.

If you already have your own personal cleansing practice and/or beauty regimen, feel free to use it. If not, or if you'd like to experiment with yours, feel free to use mine.

Deb's Beauty Regimen:

1. Set the mood in your bathroom. I always light a few candles and bath by candlelight. I also select music that will get me in the right head space.

2. Start out with a face mask. Drugstores have a wide array of them to choose from. Select one for your skin type. It's good for all genders and it will get your face super purified for the ritual. Follow the directions on the package or make your own mask. A simple one is: 1 tablespoon quick oats, half a mashed banana, 1 tablespoon milk, and 1 tablespoon of honey mixed together and applied to your face. Leave it one for fifteen minutes and then wash it off in the bath or shower.

3. Chose a soap that will be good for purifying. I tend to use Lush because they tend to have soap with salt, mud, rosemary and other natural ingredients that are good for cleansing. I have used Mud Flat Soap. (It comes back under their "Retro" category.) I have also used 13 Soap. (Discontinued. Boo!) Other good ones are:

Demon in the Dark Soap and Porridge Soap. If you would like to make your own special ritual scrub, this can be done pretty easily. Use 1/8 cup olive oil, ¼ cup coarse sea salt and 15 drops of sage essential oil and mix together.

4. Either a bath or a shower is acceptable in my opinion. A bath feels more special because most of us don't get to take a lot of them. But, a shower can be just as effective. When you are scrubbing yourself with your soap or scrub, envision scrubbing off all the negative energy that you've accumulated from day-to-day drudgery. Imagine it going down the drain.

5. If you don't have one already, get a good body scrub brush. It should have a wood or bamboo handle and natural boar bristles. They're around $10 and can be bought at an upscale grocery store or natural food store or through Amazon. After your shower, use it all over your body, always brushing towards your heart. This improves circulation and exfoliates. Don't forget the bottoms of your feet!

6. After brushing your body, moisturize your body.

7. Use toner for your face. You can either get something from Lush (I like Breath of Fresh Air.) or make your own. Get a travel-sized spray bottle and fill it ¾ full of witch hazel. Then fill it almost to the top with rose water. (It can be bought at an Indian Cash and Carry or upscale grocery store.) Add 7 drops of rose oil. Shake it before using. Then moisturize your face. I prefer either the CVS version of Olay's Complete All Day Moisturizer for Sensitive Skin or Clinque's Moisture Surge.

8. You may want to select a fragrance that is ritually appropriate to the Lady you're working with and/or the spell work you're trying to accomplish. Black Phoenix Alchemy Lab and their sister site: Twilight Alchemy Lab have a wide assortment to choose from. I use Lush's Lust perfume, BPAL's Honey Moon, TAL's Milk and Honey among others, depending on what I'm trying to accomplish.

9. If makeup is your thing, this would be where to add it. I personally try to go relatively minimal

for a ritual. I use ELF's brow shaping kit and ELF's shimmer color stick on my cheeks with Cover Girl Natural Luxe mascara and Cover Girl Natural Luxe gloss balm.

10. Time to get dressed (or not). Make sure everything is in good order.

A Day of Gathering

The French are always been lauded for their meandering shopping: meat from the boucherie,

cheese from the fromagerie, bread from the boulangerie and so on. The French also really work about five hours a day at best and food is serious business there. It's just about impossible to live like that in America unless you live in a major city. Even if you do, if you work full-time, your schedule isn't very

conducive to going to a wide assortment of shops all around town regularly.

The point of this kind of shopping isn't to exhaust you. It's to get the best of the best of everything for yourself and those you love. I can't afford it in the suburbs every week--not in time or in money. But I feel like when you are doing a ritual to a spirit who you either already have a relationship

with and thus love already or are starting a new relationship with a new spirit where you want to put out the good china to impress Her, so to speak, this is a really good time to spend some time enjoying the sensuality of gathering items for your ritual. Rituals almost always require offerings. While simple offerings are often as pleasing as elaborate offerings, this is a good time to continue to get yourself into

the ritual headspace before you even start. Go to a local farmer's market and smell the flowers and fresh fruit. Take time to select the best. Go to a bakery to select the best pastry to offer your spirit. Find the best wine or liquor to offer. Ask for recommendations from the store manager. Better yet, go to a local winery and taste for yourself. Get meat from an actual butcher. Take time to select the right cut. Go to a fabric store for a fresh swath of velvet for your altar cloth. If your spirit likes beauty items, select a gorgeous scarlet lipstick or a freshly-cut piece of soap. Everything should be the best that you can afford. (But not more than you can afford!)

Dawdle. Take your time. Enjoy the sights, sounds, and tastes of the process. It's a kind of

sensuality that American culture isn't accustomed to because it's not sex-based. It's about basking in

everything that every-day pleasures have to offer. Have a delicious cup of coffee at your favorite

coffee shop with a chocolate croissant while flipping through a magazine that makes you happy when

you're shopping for your ritual goods. The ritual preparation

process is all about changing your head

space to make it more receptive to your ritual purpose. It's also

about basking in the simple pleasures that mortal life has to offer

so that you can better understand the difference between the spirit

world

and the mortal world and where they intersect.

The Ritual Itself

What I'm offering you here is a skeleton. It's up to you to

add the sinews and the muscles to it.

I'm not a high magic magician, at heart. I'm more Jack Parsons

than Aleister Crowley. That is to say: I

think it's more useful to start building rockets in your backyard and

see what happens (while trying to

keep your fingers) rather than standing around talking about it all

day. I'm giving you my full ritual

format. But, I'm also telling you that it's meant to be tinkered with.

Try it as is to begin with, just like

you would as a novice cook with a recipe. Think about what you

liked and what you didn't like. Think

about what felt like it worked for you and what didn't. Think about

what you could do to change the

non-working parts. If your changes don't work, think about why.

Think about whether you need to

stick to the original formula or try a different change.

Yes, magic is dangerous—like science can be. Yes, there's always the chance that you could

lose fingers (or more). But, as Gordon White once told me over teacups of gin, spirits are like sharks.

You can get pretty close to a shark before it gets aggravated. You can get even closer to a shark before

it starts to think about eating you. The trick? Sharks start waving their bodies in a way that differs

from their usual "la de dah, just going about my shark business" way. They do this to let you know

they're getting pissed off so you should back off. Spirits do the same thing. If they start getting

aggravated, they're going to give you warning signs in all sorts of ways to let you know to back down.

If you think you're getting those signals, back down. Simple. And, not for nothing! While I have some small scars and skinned knees, I have yet to lose a finger because I don't stop engaging my common sense when doing magic.

This particular ritual can be performed in a group setting . I've tested it that way as well as in an

individual setting. While I am generally a group animal and generally prefer to do ritual in a group setting, I find personally that this particular ritual set up is more powerful for me to do it solo. If performing the ritual in a group setting, figure out beforehand who's doing what. Decide whether you're working from an egalitarian perspective (Everyone has equal power and is powering the ritual equally.) or from a priest/ess perspective (One person conducting the ritual while the others there assist in powering it.) Everyone needs to be on the same page ideally and "roles" should probably be assigned beforehand.

If you are using any mind-altering substances, use them before you start your working so that they have time to kick in. If you would like music for your ritual, consider making yourself a playlist for your iPod or computer or pick an album by an artist that goes along with your purpose. I use specific podcasts of A Darker Shade of Pagan or Florence + the Machine albums a lot, though I have a few playlists as well. I find it gives the noisy part of my brain something to focus on so I can focus on the ritual better.

Start by setting the altar with all the components previously listed along with any offerings you may have. Make sure you have all the spell components you may need for your work. Enscribe any chalkings or impermanent symbology you may want to use for the ritual. You will likely want to draw the shades of the room. Close the door (if possible) and purify the room using whatever methodology you prefer. I, personally, prefer using a sage smudge. Seal the door closed using a sigil of your choice and putting your will into making it a closed space that is to be undisturbed. Make sure everything you will need for the ritual is within the space where you'll be setting your circle.

Set the circle by concentrating your will on making the space the center of your own universe where you can enact magical change to your life. Using the salt, circle clockwise three times to set this space apart from the mundane. Once this is cast, you really want to avoid leaving this space until your ritual is completed for it to work best. If you're using incense, get it lit now so you're not distracted by the lighting process later. Start gathering energy for your work by chanting, singing, or drumming until you feel the power picking up in your circle. As the power picks up, chant, sing, or drum faster and faster until you feel your mind becoming attuned to the spiritual world or feel yourself starting to reach an ecstatic state. I, personally, go with the simple, *Now is the time. Now is the hour. Ours is the magic. Ours is the power.*

Next you will invoke Magic Herself. Start by telling Her about what you're offering to her. Give Her your offerings. Offer her praise and ask for Her help in opening a way for the Ladies to enter
your ritual. Ask for Her help in the magic you want to accomplish. Light Her candle and hold your
hand, wand, or knife over Her candle's flame while chanting, *Light and Dark, Light and Dark/*
Lady Magic please grant me your marque. Continue chanting until you either feel Her presence or feel
the way to the spirit world open up to you. Once you feel that, touch your tool to the part of your body

you feel is appropriate for your working (third eye, over your heart, your genitals…)

The next thing you'll be doing is building the spiritual body for your Lady to embody while taking part in your ritual. This is done by invoking the elements you have in your vessels. You can use any order you want. I usually go Earth/Air/Fire/Water. Light the candle for fire. Hold your ritual tool over the open vessel and chant, *Crowned and unbound/ Crowned and unbound/ [Fire/Water/Air/ Earth] please bring me blessings abound.* Chant until you feel that "click" that lets you know that the element you're invoking has joined your ritual.

The final invocation will be to invite the Lady you wish to work with to join your ritual. Tell Her about what you're offering to her and give Her your offerings. Offer Her praise and tell Her what you want to accomplish in your rite. Ask for Her help in the magic you want to accomplish. Light Her candle and hold your hand, wand or knife over Her candle's flame while chanting, *Heart of the Arte/ Heart of the Arte/ [Lady in Red/Lady of the Hearth/Lady of the Wood/Lady of the Mysteries]/ please come and take part.* Continue chanting until you feel Her presence. Once you feel that, touch your tool to the part of your body you feel is appropriate for your working (third eye, over your heart, your genitals…)

After you've finished your invocations, this is the place where you would do your magical working. I've made a Mojo Bag to be more Glamorous with The Lady in Red, I've enchanted my Kate Spade purse for prosperity with The Lady of the Hearth, I've enchanted my bow with The Lady of the Wood and I've scryed about my personal mysteries with The Lady of the Mysteries. I have some spells you can use in the next chapter if you're stumped. It's also more than fine to use this time to commune with the Ladies in your rite for the sake of spending time with Them. Feel free to sing, drum, dance, talk, chant, and/or meditate—all for the sake of getting to know your spirits better in lieu of a specific magical act. Obviously, you can do a magical act and spend time communing as well. Doing both would be ideal.

To further commune with the Ladies, share the drink you offered Them by drinking the small portion you poured for yourself (after pouring Their libations first) out of your cup. Bless the drink. Ask Them for a blessing or give a toast to Them. Drink.

Using your divination tool, ask your Ladies for guidance on how to continue to accomplish the magic you performed in the mundane world and future magical rites. Give yourself some time to contemplate your divination.

Thank the spirits, using the "last one in, first one out" method. Thank the Lady you invoked and snuff out her candle with a candle snuffer while chanting, *Heart of the Arte/ Heart of the Arte/ Thank you, [Lady in Red/Lady of the Hearth/Lady of the Wood/Lady of the Mysteries] for taking part.* Next, while sealing each of your vessels thank the elements you invoked by chanting, *Crowned and unbound/ Crowned and unbound/ Thank you [Fire/Water/Air/Earth] for blessings abound.* Finally, thank Lady Magic by snuffing her candle out and chanting, *Light and Dark, Light and Dark/ Lady Magic thank you for granting me your marque.*

Using your hand or foot, smudge the salt or chalking you made to start to bring your space back to mundane space. Opening the door will start to break the seal open and will start to change your head space back to daily life head space. You can either leave the door open and put your ritual items away or leave them out with the door closed overnight and then dismantle the altar in the morning.

Ritual Decompression

After a full ritual day, I'm generally not ready to completely return to daily life head space right away. You may want to develop a post-ritual ritual for slowly bringing yourself back to reality. I take off my ritual clothes and hang them up and then put on something nice and do my hair and make up for

going out. Sometimes, I smoke a clove cigarette.

I always go to the fancy restaurant/bar that's near us for happy hour with Jow. He tells me about his day and I tell him about my ritual and we "talk shop". I have a glass or two of wine and some bar appetizers. By the time we've finished, I'm in my normal, every-day, head space. Other things that are typically grounding: salt, carb-heavy food, checking your watch, doing something very mundane like writing a grocery list. (I'd check it before actually going grocery shopping!) You might try grounding meditations, talking about non-magical things with others.... Everyone has her own personal preference about how fast she wants to ground. You're captain of your own ship. You know what's best for you in this situation.

CHAPTER VI

The Arte of the Grimoire

The Arte of Charms

Tell Me I'm Pretty (Suggested for Female Identified)

Wear your sexiest Little Black Whatever. Wear an attracting perfume. Eat a fancy dessert either before or at the event. Order a glass of champagne from the most popular female bartender at the event. Order one for the bartender. Toast "To the Fairest". Tip the bartender well. Let the games begin.

Tell Me I'm Handsome (Suggested for Male Identified)

Dress to impress. Buy a wooden mala bracelet. Anoint it with an attracting oil/cologne. Before going out or at the event, have a steak dinner with a salad. Order a shot of whiskey from the most popular male bartender at the event. Order one for the bartender. Toast "To Good Hunting". Tip the bartender well. Let the games begin.

Baby Needs a New Pair of Shoes

Make a very small donation to a small local charity. Concentrate on bringing a small amount of money ($200 or less) to you from a source that is unknown to you for whatever is you need (electric bill, shoes, whatever) by giving an invocation explaining how you don't have a lot, but you are still giving freely and would appreciate a small bit of money for X in return. Use your will to manifest the specific amount of money you need. Thank your gods and spirits when it arrives.

Hire Me, Boss

Print your resume on very high quality paper. Make this your magical resume with all of your best qualities and include the salary you want and the potential job titles you want. Get a candle with St. Joseph on it from your grocery store's Latin Food section. Enscribe this resume with whatever sigils you want to use and sprinkle ground benzoin, gravel root and sea salt sprinkled on it. Roll it towards you and wrap green string around it seven times to tie it to your candle. Tie seven knots in the string. Light the candle, say the prayer on the candle the night before your interview. When you get the job, make a donation to something of St. Joseph's (St. Joseph's Hospital, St. Joseph's Church, etc.) as a thank you.

Exactly What I Was Looking For

When shopping for clothes, if you find exactly what you were looking for but it's the wrong size or color, put it back where you found it and go to another section of the store to browse. Focus on how you must have missed the right size (color, etc.) when you first looked and go back to go through the racks you left until you find the correct version.

Damsel in Distress (all genders)

If you need help with minor bureaucracy (getting a late fee waived, getting cash back for a purchase without a receipt, getting a coupon from a sales clerk, an unfamiliar charge to your account, getting a minor repair from the manufacturer, etc.), drink a cup of cinnamon tea with honey in it before you make the phone call or go to the place of business. Concentrate on being *charming* and as sweet as honey, even if you get mad. Speak softly and kindly. Ask the person how they are, compliment them. Keep explaining that you know your problem isn't their fault but you would appreciate their help with it ever so much. Keep doing this until you get what you're trying to get. Thank them profusely. Write a letter of recommendation or give a good review for the person who helped you.

Keep Your Enemies Close

If you are in a social situation where you must deal with an enemy, make sure that you are dressed your best for the occasion. The night before the event, get a candle for St. Martha from the grocery store. Light it and say the prayer on the candle. Focus on bending your enemy over to your will. Before you leave, drink a cup of peppermint tea with honey. Wear an amulet against the evil eye somewhere on your person. Bring something posh and showy for the host/ess that will ideally be shared with the gathering like champagne or beautifully plated baked brie. Be sure to kill your enemy with kindness and take the kindness offensive if possible by saying hello first, asking polite questions about their life which forces them to interact with you. You want them to underestimate you, so be soft spoken and polite.

Bag of Plenty

Pick an accessory that you use every day like a handbag, messenger bag or coat. Put a charm in the pocket that makes you think of prosperity, like a faux diamond charm from Juicy Couture or a charm that has the symbol for Mercury. Get a box of peppermint or cinnamon Altoids. Write your petition paper for the prosperity you want and fold it towards you. Put it in the box of Altoids. Awaken the spirit of your bag or coat. Offer it the Altoids and petition paper. Whenever you are offered mints at a restaurant, put them in your bag or coat. Clean the restaurant mints out regularly but keep the Altoids tin and mints unopened and unused.

For a Good Time

For a fun, sexy party without too much drama, cut a lemon in half and dip each half in sea salt. Put each half on either side of your front door. Strew your front door entrance with rosemary and rose petals. Make sure dessert and drinks have ginger, cinnamon, and/or cloves in them.

Smooth Things Out

If you are squabbling with extended family members like siblings or parents, get a candle for The Virgin of Guadalupe from your grocery store. Light the candle and recite the prayer. Have a cup of chamomile tea with a shot of mead in it and sleep on it.

I Want More

If you want to move to a higher income bracket, besides doing the obvious work of generating more income for yourself, start enchanting for the part. Put together an outfit bought on sale from a store in the income bracket you aspire to. Take a friend who is wealthier than you to a bar of a restaurant or hotel you would like to be able to afford, wearing the outfit. Buy the first round and toast to a prosperous year.

Keeping It Hot

To keep your relationship sexy, buy a set of luxury underthings. Hand wash them with a luxury hand wash detergent, rose water and a dash of Come to Me oil. Go out with your partner to a high end bar and feed each other small plates and cocktails with ginger or cinnamon in it. Go home and light red candles that are scented for attracting (honey, rose, sandalwood, etc.) in the bedroom and put your entire focus on the other person. Keep washing that set of underthings as described above.

Serial Killer Boards: Your Guide to Success

A while ago, I decided to make a serial killer board. I watch *a lot* of crime procedurals. Inevitably, a serial killer has a board that looks like what I've created – lots of yarn connecting pictures and words together. At first, Jow desperately tried to get me to stop calling it that. But he eventually succumbed to my irrefutable logic. A serial killer—at least a television fictional serial killer— has a Miss Marple level of organization and attention to detail. A TV serial killer evades being caught for a long time (usually a whole season at least). It takes a crack team of one of the best groups of CSI agents/detectives/forensic anthropologists to solve a case in about thirty-five minutes. But, the serial killer manages to stump them for twenty-five episodes. Generally, he/she can even up the ante by making the pursuit personal and killing something that this crack team loves. He/she *still* does not get caught for twenty-five episodes because of the killer's drive to succeed and attention to detail.

This fictional serial killer has a workable long-term plan. Isn't that the whole point of a focus board/success map?

Now, **I am definitely not advising you to become real-life serial killers**. Real-life serial killers aren't anywhere nearly as entertaining or as cool as the fictional ones. This is largely because of the whole morality/hurting people/having massive psychological issues/winding up with a needle in your arm and the long sleep issues. But, a fictional serial killer is created by a team of writers, very carefully, so that (if written correctly and no one is asleep on the job/phoning it in/being super half-assed about it) there are no holes in the show's plot.

And that is actually the point. There should be no plot holes in your magic. There should be measurable goals, magical work, and mundane work to make sure that your magic is doing what it's supposed to be doing. If it's not, you need to re-evaluate what you were doing and who you were working with. You need to rethink whether your goals were reasonable and achievable magically and mundanely.

A focus board is not going to do this for you.

But what it *will* do is keep your eye on the prize. In my opinion, that's the real purpose of having one. You might be easily distracted (like me) and get sidetracked from all the important shit you're actually supposed to be doing and instead watching back-to-back episodes of *Bridezillas* in your pajamas while drinking French Greyhounds. It's easy to get completely and utterly off track. That's why you need a serial killer board.

How to Be as Organized as a Television Serial Killer and Keep Your Eye on the Prize

1. First, think about what you're trying to accomplish in your life. I started by thinking of words because my brain sees words before pictures.

2. Now find pictures that you feel are good representations of what you're trying to accomplish.

3.   Get a smallish cork board and push pins. Pick a font if you want to print words. I also used good quality heavy paper for my pictures and scrapbooking scissors to cut out my pictures so they had pretty edges.

4. Arrange. This is an awesome meditative stage where you get to play god with your own life. Arrange all the pictures in a way that makes sense to you. I grouped my pictures according to each word.

5. The finishing touch. All serial killer boards have yarn connecting pictures and articles together. To be completely frank, I have no idea why that is. It looks cool? But, magically speaking, it's useful as weaving the yarn through the push pins and connecting them together can be a magical act if you use your intent. You should also think carefully about which pin to connect to which pin. For me, it was even more magical because I got to use the pink yarn that I had spun for this purpose.

6. Place the board in a location where you will often see it. If you're constantly glancing at it for a quick second at a time, then

putting the pieces together internally is more of a subconscious versus conscious act. Mine is in my office, just out of direct eyesight. This helps too. When I get bored working, I tend to look around a lot so that adds to the number of times I occasionally glance at it, often seeing a new aspect.

Dilettante Sigil Work (as given to me by Miss Spice)
Items needed:
1 eye shadow brush (or small paint brush)
1 bottle hand sanitizer (They even make them super teeny!)
Knowledge of some kind of sigil system or your imagination.

Contemplate what you are trying to accomplish. I generally want people to like me and think I'm charming (Venus) but, um, not like me too much (protection sigil). If you are feeling especially creative, think about where would be good places to place these sigils. I keep it simple by putting them on the inside of my wrists. But, you may be the creative type, in which case, maybe you want to put them over the root chakra to get laid and protective sigils on your back so your back is being watched.

Squirt a teeny tiny amount of hand sanitizer onto your eye shadow brush. If you don't like the idea of using an eye shadow brush, get a tiny paint brush. I just happen to have an eye shadow brush on me at any given time –as does Miss Spice. So, it's functional for us.

Concentrate on what you're trying to accomplish. Feel free to say some kind of chant or spell or psalm or is your personal jam I just focus and concentrate. Then, I draw the sigils on the inside of my wrists. Hand sanitizer feels cold and shows in a clear gel on your skin for a few moments so it's a good way to actualize whatever you're trying to do. I couldn't remember what sigil to use for protection and had no idea what book to find it in. So, I decided to draw a set of brass knuckles on one of my wrists. This worked perfectly. Because it's hand sanitizer and clear, it dries and no one can see it after a minute or two but you know it's there. Bonus! Clean eye shadow brush.

Steady Work Honey Pot

Items needed:

Grape seed oil

Butter melter or fragrance warmer

Coffee filter

¼-ish cup of honey

Small green taper candles

Sewing pin or needle (Remember to keep your charming and hexing needles separate.)

Bay leaf

Allspice

Cinnamon sticks

Chamomile

Irish moss

Piece of your own hair

Piece of green paper

Small jar with a lid that can handle heat

Pen

If you can manage to have a little forethought, try to do this on a Sunday, Wednesday, or Thursday during a waxing moon. You can feel smug before you even start! If not, as we say in Dianic Wicca to cover all timing issues, The Goddess is forgiving.

1. The day before, make a candle dressing oil using Kris Bradley/Mrs. B's Method
    Use:
    1/4 cup grape seed oil
    1 bay leaf
    1 teaspoon chamomile
    1 cinnamon stick (broken up)
    1 teaspoon Irish moss
    1 teaspoon allspice

Pour ingredients into the top of your scent warmer. Light candles to heat your oil all day. Let it cool. Strain with coffee filters. Store your oil in a small, Tupperware container in a cool, dark place.

2. Enscribe your candle using your pin or needle with the symbols for Mercury, Jupiter, and Fortuna Major (Geomancy). If you'd prefer to use other symbols, knock yourself out.

3. Hand tear your piece of green paper so all four edges are torn. Write steady work eight times (or, if you're a writer like me where work does not always equal payment, "steady income-generating work") without your pen leaving the paper. (I'm not great with this as yet!) Then, turn the paper 90 degrees and write your name over it. Fold the paper towards you. You can say the 23rd Psalm, if you like. I don't. I go with a simple: "So I will it, so mote it be."

4. Put your name paper in the jar. Put in three cinnamon sticks (Make sure the jar will close.), a pinch of allspice, and the lock of hair. I, personally, chose these spices because I like the way they smell and it looks aesthetically pleasing in the jar. (Oh yeah! They're good money herbs too.) Open your honey jar. Before putting it into the jar, I take a little taste. Oshun (Yoruba) likes this. Depending on your point of view and which deity, some of the Hindu pantheon like that too. (See? Look? I'm not poisoned and it's not gross! It's delightful for everyone!) I figure, if I were a goddess, I'd want human poison tasters too. Pour honey in. Close up the jar.

5. Here is the part that makes me uneasy. I recommend a small candle as it will burn out faster and save you *agita*. Light your candle and think about your steady work. Now drip some of it on

123

the top of your jar. Next, try to get your candle to stand on top of your jar's lid. Let it burn out, ideally, all the way through in one shot. If you are a nervous person like I am, I recommend having a sparkling clean kitchen sink where you can put this and it's unlikely to burn your whole house down.

6. Dress new candles and light them on the appropriate days to keep the magic going. Some people put specific time frames down for this. I am not good at that. I find it to be more helpful for me to feed a magical item when it feels like it's starting to not do its job.

How to Make a Mojo Hand

1. No more than thirteen ingredients! Keep it down in there!

2. Bag must stay hidden! At the very least, untouched by others! (If you are a lady-type who wears a bra, that's the place which is *awesome* because that's where I would stash my shaman bags. If you are a gentleman-type, a pocket is good)

3. Bag should be close to your person as much as possible or on an altar where you spend a lot of time.

4. Items in bag must be important, not just a bunch of junk you throw in there. The bag is going to be a spirit, not a junk drawer. Treat your bag accordingly! Dress the bag!

5. Remember to keep feeding the bag. (I haven't fed my Mojo Bags lately, demonstrating my usual laissez-faire-the-world-is-my-tank-of-sea-monkeys approach to life which is not good for house plants or magical workings. They will be fed tonight!)

Now a lot of bags seem to be for one purpose. My thought was: Crap! How many bags am I supposed carry around on my person? I have found it useful to have a few, single-purpose bags on altars in my house and to keep a multi-purpose bag on my person to make this issue easier.

My Process:

1. If I and (heretofore) unnamed are going to get along, I'm going to try to make it into a kindred spirit. This means having my bag drink the things I like to drink (though whiskey or rum are traditional feeding methods, spring water works well too), use colors I like...

2. The bag being flannel seems reasonably important (though not super important). Whooo! I have cute flannel fabric scraps in— OMG!!—pink. One side has little drawings of corsets and telephones and the other has pink stripes. Perfect.

3. I make a list of things I want, also referred to as: Petition papers. Some people say you should keep it a secret (like a birthday candle wish). Me? I'm not too into secret

125

traditions as a rule and I tend to believe if I'm shouting out my intentions to the universe, my success rate will be higher. I picked seven things I want because it's a magical number which may also help the bag. Once you figure out what you want to accomplish, you should gather items known to accomplish your goals. If you're not sure, check catherine yronwode's book *Hoodoo Herb and Root Magic* for suggestions. Generally speaking, a Mojo Bag is considered more powerful if you use different "kinds" of items such as herbs, stones, roots....

My bag contains (in no particular order):

a. To be pretty/thin – moonstone.
b. To have happy relationships – shallot peel (substitute for red onion).
c. To be happy – a tiny goddess with a quote about being happy on the back.
d. To save money and keep it – chamomile.
e. To have money for things I want – Irish moss.
f. To be successful in my creative endeavors – 3 bay leaves.
g. Financial stability – clear quartz.

4. I find it to be more potent if you can hand stitch your bag yourself without using a machine if possible because you're weaving your intention into the bag that way. If you're not crafty

though, a small organza wedding favor bag from a craft store will work just fine.

5. While writing your petition paper (make sure it's small and can easily fit into the bag), you may want to listen to a song that reminds you of your goals. (I chose "The Money Maker" by Rilo Kiley.) When writing your goals, make sure your pen doesn't leave the paper. It will make it look incredibly messy but that's okay. If your pen leaves the paper, start over. Fold the paper towards you.

6. Place items in the bag, making sure to charge each item appropriately.

7. Tie bag shut with yarn, cord, or... I use seven knots and I chant a part from the Pierces' song, "Sticks and Stones". (Seven times I pierce my heart/ now I feel the magic start/ bind my will and soul to keep/ so I will it/ so let it be.)

8. Dress bag with the appropriate oil for your purposes– front, back, top.

9. Gently spit good sipping Mexican tequila or the liquid of your choice onto the bag.

10. Bring the spirit to life. I think in song lyrics, so I think about the song "Bring Me to Life" by Evanescence until I

feel an excited flurry of energy from the bag. Ask your spirit what his or her name is.

11. Remember to feed your spirit who lives in the Mojo bag regularly. If you no longer want to or need to work with that bag/spirit, be sure to thank the spirit for his or her service and let the spirit know that he or she is free to leave. Then dispose of the bag and its components however is correct for your particular working.

The Arte of the Dark

A Note on the Use of the Phrase "The Dark Arts"

I am fully aware that the phrase "The Dark Arts" is featured prominently in the Harry Potter series of books. It's precisely why I use it. It's not to say I take hexing, jinxing or curse work lightly, I don't. I do it very rarely and when I do, I do it thoughtfully. But I also have a sense of humor.

On Blood and Sacrifice

Starting out as a Dianic Wiccan, the blood of choice to focus on was, of course, menstrual. While the younger prissier witches among us (myself included) turned our noses up at the idea of doing rituals involving menstrual blood, we were regaled, nonetheless, about ye olde 1970s by the older witches and their menstrual blood rituals.

128

As I aged some, I was less prissy about it and invested in a diva cup which I use regularly, to the dismay of my besties. The cup was handy to neatly pour menstrual blood from my watering can into my garden. When I had my little container garden (I do have plans to replant that next year!), I did feel a closer connection to the land. It made me feel like I was doing something sacred, something important by tending to my tiny pots (complete with tiny garden gnome) in my bare feet on my balcony. Watering them with my blood strengthened that bond too, I suppose. It didn't feel all rrrrrrrrrrrrrrrrrgh POWERFUL!!!!!!!!!! It felt nice. I don't know how else to describe it. Nice. Peaceful. I suppose, theoretically, I could have used my garden to bind everyone who set foot in my house to me in some kind of crazy Sicilian Marinara/Vaulderie Ritae. But, that wasn't really my intent. I liked feeling like something that came from me could grow something else. It made me feel linked to the land strongly and it felt, I dunno, v. circle of life somehow.

Of course, let's be real here. We all went through a phase where we wanted to be taken super-seriously in the magical community and to prove how badass we were. What's more badass to someone likely under the age of 25? Blood magic! Menstrual blood is a good starting place if you're a lady-type, but really it's not like you have to work for it. It just happens. No, there needs to be stabbing and teeth gnashing, and I don't know, whatever other tough poses you undergo when you get your finger pricked at the doctor's office. Because! It's not like it's all that easy for many of us to get serious needles. Lancets, sure. Needles, not so much. And more than that starts to get into self-harm territory. Once you realize that finger pricking is likely to be the extent of your practice and that your super manly six-year-old cousin, Andy, can handle it with a Hello Kitty Band aid and a lollipop, you need to stop and ask yourself what you're hoping to get out of it.

At the time when I first started investigating, I was more of your standard Wiccan-ish practitioner. I mean it nicely! I don't know why people get all bitchy about Wiccans anyway. They make all of us in the occult community look at least relatable to non-Pagan/Occultist/Whatever kind of special snowflake you are. Most of us at least started there. When my mother is feeling benevolent, she calls me a Wiccan instead of a godless atheist so I pretty much take it and like it. Anyway! Wiccans tended to see using blood magic as an atom bomb. Which, I suppose if you're sacrificing maidens in your backyard, it would be. Your lancet droplet of blood is more of a tiny "pew pew pew!" sort of situation.

It still seems to be strongly forbidden by most organizations. My druid organization, ADF, at one point *strongly* discouraged it. My grove being the backwater snake handlers of the tradition of course rushed to make pamphlets discussing how we are strongly discouraged (but not forbidden) to do blood sacrifice or juggle porcupines (the genesis there is a little fuzzy). Now it seems we're forbidden to do it in public ritual setting at least—which I kind of get, from a health/disease standpoint.

If you do want to do a blood sacrifice, it's best to make sure you're using a sterile lancet and to make sure you sterilize the skin and then cover the wound. *Obviously,* you shouldn't be rubbing your blood into other people's blood and you shouldn't share lancets because that's high risk behavior that could land you with HIV.

So when to use it? Okay, so it's not the toughest expression of sacrifice, and there are other expressions of sacrifice (your time, your energy, Internet time…). But it is still an expression of sacrifice. You still have to take that little tack like needle and jam it into your finger. It still hurts. It's still a tiny piece of your life force, something that is uniquely you. It's still one of the preferred personal concerns in Hoodoo.

If you can manage to contain yourself from using it for everything and keep it as a sometimes food (like cursing), that keeps it as a special kind of sacrifice. For me, I only use it when I really, really want something. I got my ex-husband housing once many many many moons ago, and I got myself the perfect rabbit burrow condo using it. I can count on one hand-ish the amount of times I've used it, I only use it when I am v. serious about something or making a v. serious offering to the land or a deity.

Some deities do like it, but if you make that an every-day food for them, be prepared to go through a lot of needles and be prepared for them to not like the idea of you breaking up with them and taking away your delicious, delicious life essence. Some deities really don't like it at all. So, do your homework before starting a teeny, dollhouse-sized blood offering for your gods.

A Tale of Curse Work and College

A while back, I foolishly agreed to teach Hoodoo 101 to the college kids in the Pagan Club at my alma mater. And I, like, promised the president that there would be absolutely no discussion on curse work. Whatsoever!

So, I'm droning about the history of Hoodoo and the differences between Hoodoo and Voodoo and how it came to our country and frankly even boring myself. The kids all were visibly twitching while having to listen to me and not being able to text or boning each other out while their roommates watch while rolling on E pills or whatever they're doing now. We all brightened up when I get to the practical applications that I had carefully redacted to be both appropriate to college kids' needs and avoiding discussion of The Dark Arts.

We chattered about fast luck and how to do well in an interview blah de blah blah. They got interested and ask about source books. Of course, I recommend cat yronwode's seminal work. However, there's not like a redacted version of it so I say vaguely that it's not all positive work so keep that in mind and I kept it moving. Much like my lazy, fat, house cats, they went from only vaguely aware of their surroundings to **HIGH ALERT! BUG! BUG! IT'S A BUG!**

Them: What do you mean?

The President:*(suspicious side eye)*

Me: Um.

Them: No, we're totally awake now and ready and willing to push back our E pill orgy and pizza party in our dorm rooms for this!

Me: The President and I spoke on this issue and it's specifically against your club's charter for me to discuss this.

The President:*(approving to me, apologetic to them)*

Them: You have said the words we have longed to hear! Forbidden knowledge! It's why we came to college! That and getting away from our smothering parents! *(They close the door and shuts the blinds like a real secret society does!)*

Me:*(Oh, Lordess! I'm boned) (looks to The President)*

The President:*(nods)*

I had a real moral quandary that I thought I had shielded myself from: Do I tell them? Or, do I let them learn about it on the streets (i.e., the Internet) where the information will be just that: information coming from a source they've never met and has no stake in their lives or even a face to them? They are adults but they're still young and impressionable in American society and frankly have probably never even read a book that even whispers about The Dark Arts. Their experience has most likely only been mostly beginner Llewellyn stuff.

I took a deep breath and I dove in.

"Okay. This is where your moral compass that we keep talking about becomes incredibly important. Karma doesn't work the way most Americans think. It's slow. It's accumulates over lifetimes. It represents both the good and the bad. While the *Law of Three* is a nice idea that's meant to keep you from getting involved in some seriously dumb stuff, it doesn't often work in a way that's observable. I can't tell you what the right thing to do is going to be for <u>you</u>. Unlike a lot of religions, most of us don't have a manual or a list of rules to follow as Pagans/Occultists. As a young adult Pagan/Occultist, it's critical that you start figuring out what you think is right and wrong now.

What are you willing to do magically, and in life? Where is your line in the sand? Whenever you work magic, you're thrusting your will over something. Do you need consent to do magic for another person? You need to decide that. You need to decide if you want to get involved with exerting your will over other people. A mentor once told me that some of the worst things she's done magically have been with good intentions and some of the best things she's done have been with bad intentions.

You also need to understand that, in Hoodoo, curse work is called a *mess* for a reason. Do not get yourself into a mess that you can't get yourself out of. I'm sure as hell not going to rush in to help you. Don't ever rush into curse work. If you're angry, you're not being sensible. It's not a good place to do curse work. You will likely do something you regret. Always give it at least three days to see if you want to tie yourself up further with the person you're angry with. Make no mistake about it! You will be tying yourself up closer with this person.

Sometimes it will be worth it. Sometimes it won't be. Sometimes your magic will work in a way you won't expect it to. Often it will, in fact. Sometimes it will work better than you wanted it to. Love spells are all fun and games until you need to get a restraining order on someone. You need to think about whether you want someone to be with you because they feel compelled to be. You need to make sure to do omen/divination work before you get involved with cursing. Bottle spells can work like this. Love spells can work like that.

Make sure you are mindful of your personal concerns. Make sure you are mindful about others' personal concerns. When I once asked a Witch what to do if you don't have them, she calmly remarked, "But why wouldn't you?"

If you're not willing to do what a curse work asks, you're likely not really ready to take that step. And that's okay. It's okay if you never work a curse in your life. But make sure you know if someone's been working on <u>you</u>. Most of the time, no one is working on you. Know the difference between crossed conditions, random bad luck, and focused ill intention. As my mentor advised: "Get a second opinion."

There is where I stand on the whole morality issue when it comes to magical gray areas. It's personal. That's part of what's both great and terrible about being part of a group of people who don't have a list of specific rules to govern us. Some of us are on board with things like love philters; some of us are appalled by it. Some of us say, well, it depends. But you need to know where you stand. You need to know where your conscience is. Only you can really dictate that for yourself as an Occultist/Pagan. It's thrilling, scary, and uncertain--just like the Universe.

When to Curse

My model is sort of *Law & Order* based. I watch a lot of procedurals when not watching reality television.

1. Egregious crime is committed against me!

2. Investigate said egregious crime. What happened? Who do I think did this, and why? What evidence do I have that this person did this? Is my own narrative correct? Cross check with someone, preferably someone who is friends with both parties and/or does not practice magic herself.

3. Do I think the Dark Arts are involved? Do I think the Dark Arts were worked against me intentionally? Check with a non-magical but magic-friendly person. (If you're too embarrassed to talk to your non-magical friend then, you're too embarrassed to curse, in my opinion.) Check with a magic-person. Do a divination. Is everyone on the same page?

4. Am I super pissed off about whatever was done to me? Better wait three days. Don't think you need to wait three days? Wait three weeks!

5. Do I think I'm a nice person?

If being thought of as a nice person by yourself and others is important to you, this isn't the best path for you. Make no mistake about what you're doing! You're intentionally harming someone. It is not a nice thing to do to someone. You are also binding yourself up with that person more closely due to the ties you're creating with this magical working. Even if you use hyssop powder. Even if you understand that karma works over life times and isn't an easily charted tit for tat process. You don't get a secret gold star for doing nasty acts on a person. It doesn't make you a "real" witch any more than anything else does. So if you're not sure, don't! Instead, I suggest a freezer spell (to follow). It's not exactly a positive energy spell but not exactly. . . not either. It's a   light shade of grey.

It's also hard to know when to stop. Why? Because you're mad, obviously! If you're mad enough at a person to want to work The Dark Arts on this person, you are probably not going to be in the best position to judge when enough is enough. Sometimes you get so mad at a person that even if s/he were set afire and eaten alive by a pack of dingoes, it still wouldn't be enough. You need a few days (or weeks) to cool off before you do any jinx work so you can assess if this is worth the aggravation. I cannot stress enough that, in Hoodoo, jinx work is called a *mess* for a reason.

If you want to have any kind of relationship with this person, you should not be performing hex work. If you want a relationship with a person, forgiveness is critical. Otherwise, you are creating a horrible toxic mess. If you need to seriously manipulate someone who is in your life in a family, friendship or romantic capacity, for things to go smoothly, you need to do some serious thinking as to why you are willing to do that over cutting that person out of your life and moving on.

6. Prepare case to go to god "court".

This is when I gather my gods and spirits to me. I plead my case and ask for their assistance and intercession. Do I get some kind of omen that they're on board? If so, continue. If not, suck it up, Buttercup. It is not that serious.

7. Commit curse work or hire an outside contractor.

If hiring an outside contractor, bear in mind that it puts Murder II on the table so to speak. In other words, while I may not have done the hit myself, but for hiring a hit person to do the deed, it would not have happened. I don't get to slither like a serpent out of it. My hands aren't clean. I need to be willing to hold myself accountable/be held accountable by my gods for it.

8. See what happens.

So, okay, in this scenario, I'm one of Jack's OMG! hot, young, plucky Assistant District Attorneys. I need to really genuinely believe in my case because I'm young and passionate and still have morals and have not yet been broken down by the system. If I really believe in my "case"/curse, I can go in with *mundi manus*, clean hands, in my own eyes. If I'm not just mad and being ridiculous, I really feel like then I am willing to commit the curse because I'm willing to put my own ass on the line with my gods and do the work to make sure this is a warranted action in the eyes of my gods.

So with all this work in mind, I hope we've established that cursing is a sometimes food and one that I've established is okay for some people to do sometimes. Now, I don't know about you, but let's take a moment to be real with ourselves. Once you learn a new trick, you want to do it for everything. Like when I first learned to do blood magic properly, suddenly everything needed a lancet involved.

Luckily, thanks to having a system in place to consider due to my complete lack of impulse control, I pondered a situation I had been pondering for quite some time. Did I want to act? I consulted Miss Spice about this situation. She pointed out that while, of course, she would support whatever psychosis I decided to engage in, perhaps it may be seen by Beings Bigger than Me (BBtM) as overkill. I decided to look into some possible actions anyway. Just some curse window shopping, you know?

And I ran into the problem I always run into when it comes to cursing. I am still unwilling to do heavy duty curse work. But more than that, it brought me to the question I always wondered: *What if you don't want to completely destroy a person? What if you just wanted to irritate her somewhere between a little and a lot?*

So what is a dilettante to do? For me, at least, I started really thinking what I wanted out of the situation past the initial impulse where I wanted fire and frogs to rain down from the sky and the person to be eaten alive by a pack of flaming (as in on fire) dingoes. So I thought on it and really tried to get to the heart of the issue. What was really gnawing at me?

In this particular situation, though I am not talking about a physical object or money or anything, I wanted back what was mine. That was it. Whatever else was the other person's, s/he could keep it. But I wanted back what was rightfully mine. So, I made sure my work was less about raining frogs and fire and more about getting back what was rightfully mine. It worked like, *comment dit-on* , a charm.

Spell Bottle Cursework

Enlist the help of your own personal deities and spirits--especially those who will be likely to be sympathetic to your case. Make them offerings. I'm assuming you're not doing this on the regular. So, make sure they're good offerings (or one half of a good offering with the promise of the second half upon delivery). State your case to them and state your intention. Be specific enough about what you want and why. But, leave some room. I promise you that the gods/spirits will be far more creative than you.

Get a bottle. If there is a kind of booze/beverage your target hates, so much the better. If not, there are a lot of really good named beers and wines that have "witchy" names. I just saw a Hex beer two days ago. Pour out the contents as a libation to your spirits.

Add nasty things like nails, needles, broken glass, vinegar, hot sauce, hot peppers and bits of items that the person hates.

You need a good personal concern from the target for this. Not a picture, not handwriting! Something good. *Good* is defined as: blood, spit, hair or semen/vaginal fluid. If you didn't have the foresight to have some of that on hand before the work and/or you don't have the chutzpah to find a way to get it, you have no business getting involved in curse work. Sorry.

Seal the bottle up.

Piss on it if you're so inclined.

Shake the bottle once a day every day for at least three days while asking your spirits for their help in what you want to happen. Make it a good speech.

Take it to the woods and hang the bottle upside down in a tree. Walk away from it and don't look back.

Mirror Box Spell Work

Enlist the help of your own personal deities and spirits--especially those who will be likely to be sympathetic to your case. Make them offerings. As in the bottle spell work, I'm assuming you're not doing this on the regular, so make sure they're good offerings (or one half of a good offering with the promise of the second half upon delivery). State your case to them and state your intention. Be specific enough about what you want and why but leave some room. I promise you that the gods/spirits will be far more creative than you.

Make a very small poppet of the person, dressing it with personal concerns. As with the bottle spell, again, **you need a good personal concern from the target for this.** Not a picture, not handwriting! Something good. *Good* is defined as blood, spit, hair or semen/vaginal fluid. If you didn't have the foresight to have some of that on hand before the work and/or you don't have the chutzpah to find a way to get it, you have no business getting involved in curse work. Sorry.

Get a small wooden box from a craft store. Glue tiny mirrors from the craft store inside the box.

Bind the poppet up with some string and tell it why you are mad at the target. Tell it that, every time the target speaks badly of you or tries to do something bad to you, their words/actions will be reflected back at the target. Some people say that this will make the person crazy if it gets reflected often enough—which is why it's not a nice thing to do.

Put the poppet in the box. Go to the woods. Find a large rock or brick and put it on top of the box. Put your foot on top of it. Say, "I have you [Target's full name] under my heel." Walk away. Don't turn back.

Freezer Spell

This jinx is to "freeze" someone out of your life permanently and to stop this person from acting against you. If you have any hope of reconciliation with this person, do not do this spell!

Because this is a much lesser jinx (in the version that I am teaching you), you don't need quite as strong personal matter. A picture or the target's name in the person's handwriting will suffice.

Write your petition paper with the person's name and what you want to freeze that person out of. (For example: "I want to freeze Anita Smith out of my personal life.") Don't let your pen leave the page. Put the picture or their handwriting on top of the petition paper and a little chia seed (to stop gossip) on top. Fold the paper away from you while saying, "I'm giving you the freeze/ stay away from me, please." Wrap the packet up in purple (to show your control over the situation) ribbon.

Use sea salt and a little water to wet the packet (about 1/8 cup) and put it in a Ziploc bag. Put it in the back of your freezer. Keep it in there as long as you feel you need to keep the person on "ice". When you're done with it, dispose of it at a crossroads. Note that disposing of the materials doesn't break the spell work but the work won't be as "active" at that point either.

Magic Based Recipes for Eating and Spell Work

A Super Quick American Style Puja

* Tell Ganesha he is a benevolent elephant and he's awesome.
* Light a small ghee lamp (a little clay pot, a dab of ghee and a cotton wick, you can get it at an Indian Cash & Carry) and thank Agni for the fire.
* Ring a bell.
* Put a tiny ramekin-sized bit of food for Shiva and Parvati on your altar. (Use the recipe below. Shiva's family will accept it—in my experience. Adding some dried fruit and pretty candies to the side of the plate helps the cause.)
* Talk up the food like a waitress. (I've said for a while that that's what I want my magical title to be: Divine Waitress.)
* Tell Them how awesome both of Them are.
* Ask for Them to help you have a good relationship with your significant other. (It helps if you've been working with Them and doing Japa practice in addition to this.)

* Take kum kum powder off your idol or picture and put new kum kum powder on Their feet and heads.
* Ring bell again.
* Eat dinner.

Chicken Lentil Curry: Lazy American Style

Ingredients

1 can or box of lentil soup

2 chicken thighs, cut into pieces. Leave the skin on or take it off.
It's your business.

2 small onions, chopped

2 teaspoons ghee or butter

2 tablespoons curry (or to taste)

1 tablespoon garam masala

1/4 teaspoon ground ginger

1/4 teaspoon cumin

1/4 teaspoon turmeric

1 pouch instant rice. (Take it out of the pouch to put into the soup.)

Put butter into the pot and melt it on medium heat. Put the onions
and chicken in and brown. Add in the the rest of the ingredients.
Let cook for approximately 20 minutes.

Finished!

Roasted Chicken Dinner For Goddesses and Mortals Alike

I roast a whole chicken on a week night. Darlings, roasting is your
friend. It's even lazier than crock potting, in my opinion. I got a
whole, five-pound, organic chicken for like $6 at my grocery store.
This is a huge steal. It was dinner for Jow and me, one night, lunch
for Jow for the week and then I used the bones and such for stock.
Cooking a whole chicken is super easy and super frugal. It can be

used as a devotion to the Goddess, too. You can pick a particular goddess if you like. But, my lazy reclaimist roots are showing here. You can do the heavy lifting on your own, sport. The way this ritual is set up is so that as you are infusing your chicken. When you eat it, you will be likewise infused. Usually I don't taste it when poultry is stuffed with something. But, I definitely do with this recipe.

1 whole three-to-five-pound chicken completely defrosted (ideally at room temperature).

1/2 bunch of thyme

1/2 lemon

1 head of garlic, cut in half (NOT peeled or anything)

1 container of fresh Brussels sprouts (or some other roast-able vegetable. I won't tell the kitchen police on you!)

1 packet of powder chicken gravy

2 tablespoons butter

Salt and pepper to taste

Roasting pan

1 white candle

Take three deep breaths to focus. As you are lighting the candle say, "Great Goddess, please bless me with your presence here in my hearth." Or whatever you like! Again, I'm not the kitchen/Goddess police.

Preheat your oven to 425. Take your chicken out of the package and remove any plastic that's on your chicken (holding the legs together or whatever). Now, this is where you're going to get reeeeally close to your chicken. The cavity is located between its legs. You're going to take off whatever jewelry you have on your hand and wrist and reach into that cavity and pull out whatever treats they've stuffed in there for you (probably the neck and the gizzards) and pull them out. You can do whatever you like with them, I usually toss them.

Feeling close to your chicken? Good. Now you are going to loosen the skin by the cavity so that the skin is not attached to the meat on the top of the breast and bottom of the chicken. You're going to carefully stuff about half a teaspoon of butter in between the skin and the meat on each side without ripping the skin. I'm lazy and can never find my pastry brush, so I rub butter with my fingers all over the chicken. Use as little or as much as you want. Go crazy.

Wash your hands with soap and concentrate on making it a little hand washing purification to the Goddess. You can put a little table salt in your hands while you're washing them to make that so.

Take your thyme and run it over the candle. Touch the thyme to your heart and say, "Great Goddess, beautifully crowned, keep my home safe and sound. Make me strong. Keep me from doing what's wrong."

Put it inside the cavity.

Take your garlic halves and run them over the candle. Touch the garlic halves to your heart and say, "Great Goddess, shining bright, help me fight the good fight."

Put it inside the cavity.

Take your lemon halves and run them over the candle. Touch the lemon half to your heart and say, "Great Goddess above, infuse me with your love."

Put it inside the cavity.

Say, "By the power of three times three, so I will it so mote it be."

Put the chicken into your roasting pan. Try to tuck the wings under as best as you can. Trim your Brussels sprouts and surround the chicken with them. Cook for one hour, but make sure the juices run clear. Fish out Brussels sprouts. Carve in the roasting pan if possible, so you have the juices. Remove chicken pieces and carcass (with the stuffed ingredients) from the pan. Add the chicken gravy powder and about half a cup of water. Stir until not lumpy. Pour into a gravy boat. Microwave for one minute.

Put the carcass and items inside the carcass into your crock pot. Add whatever odds and ends you have in your fridge: limp parsley, old carrots that haven't gone off yet, celery that's lying around not doing anything... No chopping is needed. Fill the crockpot with water. Cook on low until morning. Strain. Then put the stock into very small Tupperware containers so that it's easily accessible and defrost-able. Freeze.

After you're done cooking, either let the candle burn out by itself or extinguish with a candle snuffer saying, "Great Goddess, I thank you for your presence."

Dinner is served. I made stove top stuffing to go with it because it's super easy. You can do whatever you want.

Prosperity Pasta Avec Parsley and Dill

Parsley is good for protection and money drawing and love and dill is good for money and hex breaking. So, you can cover all your magical bases with the two herbs used and can enchant as you see fit as it covers the four main bases of magic. This recipe is quick and economical as well!

1 box pasta (We like pastina or elbows.)
4 tablespoons butter
Palm full of grated Parmesan cheese
1 handful of fresh chopped parsley
1 handful of fresh chopped dill
salt and pepper to taste

Cook pasta according to the directions. Drain. Add the rest of the ingredients. Et Voila! Dinner est served!

Aphrodisiac Chocolate Quick Bread

You can make this bread to keep your lover interested in you, as a devotional to Aphrodite or Erzulie, or to sweeten someone's disposition toward you.

6 tablespoons 2% milk

1/3 cup low fat sour cream

1 room temperature egg

3 teaspoons honey

8 tablespoons sugar

1 cup white whole wheat flour

1/2 teaspoon baking powder

1/4 teaspoon baking soda

1/2 teaspoon salt

1/2 teaspoon vanilla extract

1/2 cup chocolate chips

Put the ingredients in the order listed into your bread machine. Select small loaf, light crust and use the quick bread setting. In a little more than an hour you'll have the bread

Stuffed Pumpkin for Samhain

I find that Samhain really kicks off the start of holidays with a bunch of people jammed into a house that you wish you could escape. Sadly, I am far too masochistic to take the far more reasonable misanthropic solitary approach to the holidays. So to my grove I go, pumpkin in hand! I find food helps make up for personal social awkwardness. It acts as a pre-emptive apology. "Sorry I can't feign interest in the boring topic you have trapped me into conversation about. I made you a pumpkin!" At the very least, I can always be grateful that Samhain is hosted at our Señora Druid's house, enabling me to leave before I turn into a pumpkin and/or say or do something that brings dishonor to my family. Oh! I don't cook like this for every Sabbat because that leads to heavier drinking and high coven mate expectations—which should both be avoided. This is my big "ta-da" for the year.

1 large cheese pumpkin (the light orange kind)

1 box cornbread mix

3 stalks celery, diced

1 carrot, diced

2 shallots, diced

1 pack Italian turkey sausage

2 cups chicken stock

3 tablespoons fresh sage, chopped

1 large aluminum roasting pan

olive oil

1 teaspoon fresh rosemary, chopped

Make the cornbread according to the directions on the box the night before. Cut cooled corn bread into small cubes. Leave out overnight.

Delegate. Carving open the top of the pumpkin is a huge pain in the butt. Find another sucker who doesn't mind potentially losing fingers to the surly pumpkin. Make sure the diameter of the opening is almost as large as the top of the pumpkin. A cheese pumpkin puts up a bigger fuss than a regular pumpkin on being carved so make sure your special helper uses a very sharp implement.

Scoop out pumpkin guts. Cheese pumpkins have fewer seeds and fewer guts. Have your special helper pick out the seeds.

Preheat your oven to 250 degrees.

Mix seeds with a teaspoon of salt, pepper and fresh chopped rosemary and 3 capfuls of olive oil. Spread out on a baking sheet.

Gently score the inside of the pumpkin with a knife. Brush olive oil on the inside and outside of the pumpkin. Salt and pepper the inside.

Put the pumpkin in its pan and put it and the seeds in the oven.

Move the seeds around every ten minutes until they are to your desired crispiness and then remove from the oven.

Roast the pumpkin for an hour.

While the pumpkin is roasting, warm up 2 capfuls of olive oil in a frying pan. De-case the sausage by squishing it out of its casing like a tube of toothpaste. Crumble it into the frying pan with the carrot, celery and shallots. Cook until vegetables are softened and the sausage is browned.

In a mixing bowl, mix sage, chicken stock, vegetables, corn bread and sausage together. Salt and pepper.

Put stuffing into pumpkin. Roast for another 30 minutes.

Afterword

A Love Letter (of sorts) to My Muse

Writing this book really started as a dare from my Muse. Muses are fickle, disorderly creatures. (That is why so many artists have such a hard time making a living from their art.) Mine always reminds me of Serena Vander Woodsen after a bender on *Gossip Girl*. We have a contentious relationship, at best. I'm the roommate just after college with a chore wheel and a 9-5 who's in bed by ten and has her clothes picked out for the next day. She's the roommate who rolls in at 4 in the morning on a Tuesday, half empty bottle of Veuve Clicquot champagne in hand, new Cartier bauble around her neck, smelling of an imported Gruyere grilled cheese sandwich from a gourmet food truck. She has no actual discernible job. She's late with the bills. She has a capricious temper, and she sure as hell doesn't do dishes. You can see why we don't get along. Muses hate punching a clock. Your survival depends on being able to work in an orderly fashion.

If you're something like me, half marketing idiot savant, half artiste, you can learn to make a go of it. You learn to not depend on her. You even learn to ignore her. You may not be as talented as some. But you know how to hold down a day job that helps you lead a tidy middle-class American existence. You work at your skills as a crafter and learn to get better, faster. You learn pricing. You learn how to market. You learn how to make headway on Etsy. You learn the best sources for material purchasing. You learn the best shows to do. You learn how to network with your fellow crafters. you figure out what sells best. With crafting, while there are spurts of inspiration (more the marketing kind than the artistic genius kind, to be frank), it's easier to regard it as a job. People exchange money for your goods and services. It's recognizable. Respectable even.

But crafting isn't writing. I've been able to write and be published in a reasonable manner, with only the occasional tiny bit of attention from my Muse. So when my Muse busted down my door after midnight on a Tuesday right before Christmas of 2011, I didn't know the extent to which my life would change. I think if I had, I would have fought her harder. She shoved me down the rabbit hole for twenty-three weeks where I led my first eCourse, *New Year, New You: An Experiment in Radical, Magical Transformation*. I struggled alongside my students as we did our best to make our own luck in 2012. I wrote, every week. I learned to write during the naptimes of my tiny charges that I nannied for on borrowed laptops. I wrote when I was sick; I wrote when I was well. I wrote when I had a lot to say and I wrote when I felt like I had nothing to say. I took the journey with my students and it's what has led me to here.

I've called myself a writer for a long time. But, I still hesitate to call myself an author. To me, a writer writes small things that do not make up one whole book. An author writes books. And in the interest of full disclosure (because I've been a blogger for the last ten years, I sort of don't know how to not vomit up most of my feelings on any given situation), that's where I've always choked. I've written outlines. I've written first chapters. I've even written the first third of a book! But, inevitably, I choke.

It doesn't matter if it's romance, young adult fiction, or non-fiction. It's what always happens. I start to think, *maybe next year.* And I go back to doing what's comfortable. I'm pretty good at the things I'm pretty good at. I write my blog entries, my witty little articles, and an occasional short story or freelance piece. But there's a silent judgment from my Muse when we pass each other in the halls that I will never be a real author until I have a book that is completely mine.

Dear S.,

I don't like you. I don't know that I ever will. You're everything I rally against. You wreck my world view. You're an agent of chaos. In case you haven't figured it out, I hate chaos. Maybe you have. Maybe it's why you're not home much. I can understand that. I wouldn't want someone pissing on my parade at every given opportunity when all I've tried to do is help.

Maybe you figure the only way to get me to listen is to employ the guerilla tactics that you've employed. It's hard to ignore someone standing at your bedside at one in the morning on a week day, kicking the bed until you wake up. I know you hate to be ignored. Presumably, it's taken you this long to realize I was ignoring you instead of the other way around as you prefer. I'm sure I'm just as frustrating for you as you are to me. Seeing me dither around with boring things like a day job and house cleaning and lying on the couch like a zombie, too exhausted to even remember what inspiration looked like. I'm sure you didn't want the other Muses to think that your girl was a spectacular failure. They'd all sit around laughing at you and how much your charge sucked. It would make for awkwardness for you at Butter at oh-mi-god o'clock.

However, this sadomasochist relationship we're in is difficult for me. It's really hard for me to be who you want me to be. I know what you want and I know you won't stop until you get it-- even if it runs me into the ground. Even if it kills me. Muses aren't born with a lot of compassion. Compassion doesn't make for artistic work. I know, without you, I'd be lazy and unfulfilled, living a stupid suburban existence that we both hated when I was sixteen and we were more on the same page. When I used to run with you. When we used to be friends. Sisters. So I'm doing this for you. To make you proud of me. So that we both know I didn't just kill everything that I loved when I grew up. I will birth this book for you—out of blood, keyboard and tea. You'll smile at me and I'll smile at you. And, for a moment, a brief shining moment, we'll be exactly on the same page again and everything will be right.
I love you—as much as I hate you.
D.

About Deb and Final Thoughts on Using This Book

A bit of ego is necessary for all artists really. If you want to be an artist of any kind, you need some egotism to believe that others will share your belief in your vision/ (perhaps over the vision of others) and pay you money for the privilege.

Getting to the point where I believed in myself enough to write my own book has taken thirty-three years. I figured JC started a religion that has lasted a couple thousand years at my age, the least I could do is write the damn book already!

I'm telling you all this so that you know that this wasn't something that came naturally or easily for me. I'm writing right now with my heart in my throat and my squishy bits on my sleeve. I've been in a state of cold fear since the Experiment was winding down because I knew I couldn't put it off any longer. So I set things up to make it so that I wouldn't lose momentum and I would just springboard from one project to this and everything would be nice and tidy. I think it goes without saying that this has been anything but tidy so far. I've been sick (I think my sinuses are broken), craft season is under way (so much schlepping and spinning), I'm attempting to still blog (Can't lose my loyal audience!), my tiny charges have been sick (which means naps can only happen flopped between my breasts and tummy), and Jow and I are getting married in September (Stag and Hen parties! Bridal showers! Lingerie shopping!). It's a lot. Sometimes, I think that I was crazy to ever think this was even going to ever be possible.

This is supposed to be the year where all things are supposed to be possible. Where I make my destiny, as per my Muse that faithful week night right before Christmas. It seemed like a great idea when the Intertubes had a warm holiday glow about the blogosphere. I was drinking a lot of French Greyhounds at the time and feeling very inspired about the whole situation, inspiring the blogosphere for a heady week to climb aboard.

It's significantly less inspiring now in June, snotting my brain out through my nose hunched over a computer alone in sweats at a kitchen table, completely sober. There are other books I could have written. Easier, less personal books in other fields. But, for whatever reason, my Muse was insistent that this particular book should be my first. I've written other outlines for Kitchen Witch books that were a slightly hipper version of your standard issue recipe treasury, with some basic magic thrown in. I thought I was going to be the new occultist Rachel Ray or something. That would have been safer and less vulnerable. I've chosen instead to share with you the way that I do magic and the way I see magic. This is, frankly, more personal for me than asking you to go to bed with me. In my other life, I write lurid and graphic sex scenes in my romantica work. That is less squishy than this. It's easy for me to talk and write about sex. At the end of the day, it's mechanics and choreography with a little bit of feeling talk thrown in. I don't want to go through the book having to disclaim everything so I will just say it once here. You don't have to agree with everything I say and do in this book. Lordess knows I never do when reading nonfiction! I'm not the magic police. I'm not in your ritual space breathing down your neck telling you to do everything exactly the way that I do it. If you tweak something or only use a part of something and it works for you, awesome.

You'll know pretty loud and clear if it doesn't work.

I've been developing my view on magic for almost half my life. My background includes Dianic Wicca, Hoodoo, ADF Druidry, Neo-Shamanism, Hinduism in a Pagan context and Hearth Witchery. I've participated in the Amethyst Circle of Sisters for almost half my life and Grove of the Other Gods for almost as long. I've been blogging about my magical adventures for the last several years at my blog, *Charmed, I'm Sure.*

I live in New Jersey with my husband-elect, Jow. He will be my actual husband by the time this goes to publication. We cohabitate with our two cats. I have my degree in Women's Studies/Psychology. I was an administrative assistant for most of my professional life. I find I'm enjoying myself as a nanny as my day job. In my "spare" time, I'm launching my crafting business on Etsy (La Sirene & Le Corbeau and The Glamoury Apothecary) and in my local community. I like St. Germain cocktails and watch too much reality television.

A Parting Shot

I hope that you've found this book useful in bringing more glamour to your everyday life and your magical life. It's been a huge personal journey for me and the act of writing this has brought more glamour to my life personally. Through writing this book, I've learned so much! I have a regular ritual practice, I can put on eye makeup competently and my house doesn't look like a hurricane just blew through it.

would like to thank my mom, Frances Castellano for believing in me as an author since I was a little girl with a pink notebook and for holding my hand through this whole process even when I cried (a lot). I love you, Mom!

There's not enough praise in the world for my husband, Joseph Scangarella. I would have never started blogging about my magical practice if he didn't suggest it. He has read everything I've written and commented thoughtfully no matter how many times I needed reassurance. He has done so many dishes and taken so many trips to the post office and made so much dinner for me and has never given up on me. I know how much you've sacrificed for this, darling Jow. I love you more than a sea of stars.

Gordon White deserves so many thanks for being my platonic European husband and believing in me and putting my hands to the fire, no matter how much I was screaming. I needed it!

Thank the gods for my editor, Gail Lennon who knew what I was trying to say even when I didn't. She kept me on track and pushed me to believe in myself and this book when I needed it most.

Finally, I would like to thank my best girls – Brenna Barkley, April Rucker, Danielle Drust and Miss Spiceand my best writing partner, John Minus. You all have been there for me so much and have listened and read and poured the wine. You always had an unshakable faith that I would be able to finish writing a book. I did it! I love you!

CPSIA information can be obtained
at www.ICGtesting.com
Printed in the USA
LVHW090005031120
670542LV00006B/483